Vegetarian

A classic kitchen collection for the busy cook

£1-50 05/26

MURDOCH BOOKS

Contents

12 **Mushrooms with herb nut butter**

11 **Pumpkin pesto bites**

14 **Potato and olive scones**

22 Grilled vegetables with garlic mayonnaise

26 Baked ricotta

Snacks and starters

Spinach pies

»PREPARATION 25 MINUTES »COOKING TIME 20 MINUTES »MAKES ABOUT 20

1 Put the yeast and sugar in a bowl with 60 ml (2 fl oz/¼ cup) of warm water. Leave in a warm, draught-free place for 10 minutes, or until bubbles appear on the surface. The yeast mixture should be frothy and slightly increased in volume. If the yeast doesn't foam, it is dead, so discard it and start again.

2 Sift the flour into a bowl, then add the yeast mixture, 2 tablespoons of the olive oil and 185 ml (6 fl oz/ ¾ cup) warm water. Mix to form a dough, then turn out onto a lightly floured board. Knead for 10 minutes until smooth and elastic. Put the dough into an oiled bowl and leave in a warm, draught-free place for up to 2 hours, until doubled in size.

3 Preheat the oven to 190°C (375°F/Gas 5), and grease two large baking trays. Wash the spinach, leaving a generous amount of water on the leaves. Put the spinach in a saucepan, cover and cook over high heat until wilted. Drain the spinach in a colander, squeezing against the sides to remove the excess water. Roughly chop the spinach.

4 Heat 1 tablespoon of the olive oil in a frying pan and cook the onion and garlic until softened. Put in a bowl with the spinach, pine nuts, lemon juice and zest. Season with the nutmeg and some salt and pepper. Set aside to cool.

5 Turn the dough onto a floured board and knock down. Divide into balls the size of an egg and roll each into a 10 cm (4 inch) round. Place 1 tablespoon of filling in the centre of each round. Brush the edges of the rounds with water, then bring up the sides at three points to form a triangle, pressing the edges to seal. Place on the trays, leaving room for the pies to spread as they cook. Brush them with beaten egg and bake for 15 minutes, until golden. Serve hot.

Note Toast the pine nuts in a dry frying pan over medium heat, stirring constantly, until they are golden brown and fragrant. Watch carefully as they will burn easily.

- 2 teaspoons dried yeast
- 1 teaspoon sugar
- 375 g (13 oz/3 cups) plain (all-purpose) flour
- 60 ml (2 fl oz/¼ cup) olive oil
- 750 g (1 lb 10 oz) English spinach, trimmed
- 1 large onion, finely chopped
- 1 garlic clove, crushed
- 80 g (2¾ oz/½ cup) pine nuts, toasted (see Note)
- 2 tablespoons lemon juice
- 1 teaspoon finely grated lemon zest
- ¼ teaspoon ground nutmeg
- 1 egg, lightly beaten

Baked polenta with spicy relish

»PREPARATION 20 MINUTES »COOKING TIME 1 HOUR »MAKES 48

600 ml (21 fl oz) milk
100 g (3 1/2 oz/2/3 cup) polenta (see Note)
25 g (1 oz) butter, diced
1 tablespoon olive oil
1 tablespoon polenta, extra

Spicy relish
2 red onions
500 g (1 lb 2 oz) roma (plum) tomatoes
1 tablespoon oil
1 large red chilli, finely chopped
1/4 teaspoon Mexican chilli powder, or to taste
1 tablespoon soft brown sugar
1 tablespoon red wine vinegar

1 Lightly grease a 20 x 30 cm (8 x 12 inch) cake tin. Bring the milk to the boil in a saucepan. Reduce the heat to medium and then whisk in the polenta, pouring it in a stream, until it thickens. Stir constantly with a wooden spoon for 20 minutes, or until the polenta leaves the side of the pan. Remove from the heat and stir in the butter. Season to taste.

2 Spread the polenta into the tin and smooth the top. Refrigerate for 2 hours, or until set.

3 To make the spicy relish, roughly chop the onions and tomatoes. Heat the oil in a frying pan, then add the onion and cook, stirring, over high heat, for 3 minutes. Add the tomato, chilli, chilli powder, brown sugar and vinegar. Simmer, stirring occasionally, for 20 minutes, or until thickened. Season with salt.

4 Preheat the oven to 200°C (400°F/Gas 6). Turn the polenta out onto a board, cut into 5 cm (2 inch) squares, then into triangles. Put the polenta on a baking tray covered with baking paper, brush with the olive oil and sprinkle with the extra polenta. Bake for 10 minutes, or until the polenta is golden and has a crust. Serve hot or warm with the warm relish.

Note You can also use instant polenta, which only takes about 3 minutes to cook.

Potato samosas

»PREPARATION 20 MINUTES »COOKING TIME 40 MINUTES »MAKES 16

1 Finely dice the potatoes. Heat the oil in a large heavy-based frying pan and cook the potato and ginger over medium heat for 8 minutes, stirring constantly. Add the cashew nuts, shredded coconut, coconut cream and coriander, stir to combine and season. Leave to cool.

2 Cut each pastry sheet into four. Place quarter cupfuls of the filling in the centre of each square, then brush the pastry edges with water. Press the edges together, twist to seal, then chill for 15 minutes.

3 Fill a large heavy-based saucepan one-third full of oil and heat the oil to 180°C (350°F), or until a cube of bread dropped into the oil browns in 15 seconds. Cook the samosas in batches for 6 minutes, or until they are golden and crisp. Drain on paper towel and serve immediately with a dip made from plain yoghurt, finely chopped cucumber, chopped chilli and perhaps some chopped mint, if desired.

3 all-purpose potatoes
1 tablespoon olive oil
2 teaspoons chopped ginger
90 g (3¼ oz) roasted cashew nuts, chopped
15 g (½ oz/¼ cup) shredded coconut
60 ml (2 fl oz/¼ cup) coconut cream
3 tablespoons chopped coriander (cilantro) leaves
4 sheets shortcrust (pie) pastry
oil, for deep-frying

Sticky rice pockets

»PREPARATION 1 HOUR »COOKING TIME 2 HOURS »MAKES 20

1 Soak the dried bamboo leaves in boiling water for 10 minutes, or until soft. Drain.

2 Meanwhile, chop the spring onions and water chestnuts. Cut the eggplant into 1 cm (½ inch) cubes.

3 Heat half the oil in a wok and swirl to coat the base and side. Cook the spring onion and eggplant over high heat for 4–5 minutes, or until golden. Stir in the water chestnuts, mushroom soy sauce, chilli, sugar and coriander. Leave to cool.

4 Bring 750 ml (26 fl oz/3 cups) water to a simmer in a saucepan. Heat the remaining oil in a separate saucepan, add the rice and stir for 2 minutes, or until coated. Add 125 ml (4 fl oz/½ cup) of the hot water and stir over low heat until it is all absorbed. Repeat until all the water has been added — this should take about 20 minutes. Add the soy sauce and white pepper.

5 Fold one end of a bamboo leaf on the diagonal to form a cone. Hold it securely in one hand and spoon in 2 tablespoons of the rice. Make an indent in the rice, add 1 tablespoon of the eggplant filling, then top with another tablespoon of rice. Fold the other end of the bamboo leaf over to enclose the filling, then secure with a toothpick. Tie tightly with kitchen string. Repeat with the rest of the bamboo leaves and filling.

6 Put the rice parcels in a single layer in a double bamboo steamer. Cover with a lid and sit over a wok half filled with simmering water. Steam for 1½ hours, or until the rice is tender, adding more boiling water to the wok as needed. Serve hot.

Notes Bamboo leaves are used to wrap food before cooking, but they are not eaten.

Mushroom soy sauce is available from Asian food stores.

- 20 dried bamboo leaves (see Notes)
- 6 spring onions (scallions)
- 80 g (2¾ oz/½ cup) drained water chestnuts
- 400 g (14 oz) eggplant (aubergine)
- 125 ml (4 fl oz/½ cup) oil
- 1 tablespoon mushroom soy sauce (see Notes)
- 3 small red chillies, seeded and finely chopped
- 2 teaspoons sugar
- 3 tablespoons chopped coriander (cilantro)
- 800 g (1 lb 12 oz/4 cups) white glutinous rice, washed and well drained
- 2 tablespoons soy sauce
- 1 teaspoon ground white pepper

Pumpkin pesto bites

»PREPARATION 20 MINUTES
»COOKING TIME 35 MINUTES »MAKES 48

1 Preheat the oven to 200°C (400°F/Gas 6). Peel 750 g (1 lb 10 oz) of butternut pumpkin (squash) and cut it into 2 cm (¾ inch) slices, then into rough triangular shapes about 3 cm (1¼ inches) along the base. Toss with 1 tablespoon oil, some salt and some cracked black pepper until coated. Spread the pumpkin on a large baking tray and bake for 35 minutes, or until tender.

2 Meanwhile, to make the pesto, put 35 g (1¼ oz/¼ cup) roasted hazelnuts, 35 g (1¼ oz) rocket (arugula), 1 tablespoon freshly grated parmesan and 30 ml (1 fl oz) oil in a food processor, and process until they form a paste. Season well.

3 Spoon a little hazelnut pesto onto each piece of baked pumpkin and sprinkle with 2 tablespoons freshly grated parmesan cheese and some black pepper. Serve warm or cold.

Olive basil cheese spread

»PREPARATION 15 MINUTES »COOKING TIME NIL »MAKES 500 G (1 LB 2 OZ/2 CUPS)

1 Combine 250 g (9 oz/1 cup) softened cream cheese, 200 g (7 oz) feta cheese, 20 g (¾ oz) basil leaves, and 1 tablespoon olive oil in a bowl. Mix until smooth. Add ¼ teaspoon cracked black pepper.

2 Pit and chop 15 Kalamata olives and fold into the cheese mixture. Spoon into a serving bowl, smooth the top with the back of the spoon and pour 2 tablespoons olive oil over the top. Garnish with a little more cracked pepper. Serve with warm bruschetta.

Cheese and curry lentil balls

»PREPARATION 15 MINUTES »COOKING TIME 20 MINUTES »MAKES ABOUT 30

1 Put 250 g (9 oz/1 cup) red lentils in a saucepan and cover with water. Bring to the boil, reduce the heat, cover and simmer for 10 minutes, or until tender. Drain.

2 Put half the lentils in a food processor with 4 chopped spring onions (scallions) and 2 crushed garlic cloves. Process until smooth. Transfer to a large bowl, then stir in the remaining lentils, 1 teaspoon ground cumin, 80 g (2¾ oz/1 cup) fresh breadcrumbs, 125 g (4½ oz/1 cup) grated cheddar cheese and 1 large grated zucchini (courgette). Roll level teaspoons of the mixture into balls and toss lightly in polenta.

3 Fill a heavy-based saucepan one-third full of oil and heat the oil to 180°C (350°F), or until a cube of bread dropped into the oil browns in 15 seconds. Cook the lentil balls in small batches for 1 minute, or until golden and crisp. Drain on crumpled paper towel. Serve hot.

Mushrooms with herb nut butter

»PREPARATION 20 MINUTES »COOKING TIME 20 MINUTES »SERVES 4–6

1 Preheat the oven to 180°C (350°F/Gas 4). Grease a shallow ovenproof dish with oil or melted butter. Remove the stalks from the mushrooms. Put the mushroom caps in the dish and finely chop the stalks. Heat the oil in a small frying pan. Cook the onion over medium heat for 2–3 minutes, or until soft and golden. Add the mushroom stalks. Cook for 2 minutes, or until softened. Remove from the heat.

2 Put the almonds, garlic, lemon juice, parsley, thyme, rosemary, chives, butter, ½ teaspoon salt and ¼ teaspoon pepper in the bowl of a food processor and process for 20–30 seconds, or until smooth.

3 Place the mushroom caps in the ovenproof dish. Spoon the onion and mushroom mixture into each cap and smooth the surface. Top each mushroom with the herb and almond mixture and bake for 10–15 minutes, until the mushrooms are cooked through and the butter has melted.

Note Mushrooms are best cooked just before serving. Assemble the caps up to 2 hours before serving and store, covered, on a flat tray, in the refrigerator.

12 large mushrooms
1 tablespoon olive oil
1 small onion, finely chopped
40 g (1½ oz) blanched almonds
1 garlic clove, chopped
1 tablespoon lemon juice
3 tablespoons parsley sprigs
3 teaspoons chopped thyme or 1 teaspoon dried thyme
3 teaspoons chopped rosemary or 1 teaspoon dried rosemary
1 tablespoon snipped chives
75 g (2¾ oz) butter, chopped

Dolmades

»PREPARATION 1 HOUR »COOKING TIME 1 HOUR 15 MINUTES »MAKES 50

125 ml (4 fl oz/½ cup) olive oil
6 spring onions (scallions), chopped
150 g (5½ oz/¾ cup) long-grain rice
15 g (½ oz) chopped mint
2 tablespoons chopped dill
170 ml (5½ fl oz/⅔ cup) lemon juice
35 g (1¼ oz/¼ cup) currants
40 g (1½ oz/¼ cup) pine nuts
235 g (8½ oz) packaged vine leaves (about 50)
2 tablespoons olive oil, extra

1 Heat the oil in a saucepan. Add the spring onion and cook over medium heat for 1 minute. Stir in the rice, mint, dill and half the lemon juice. Season to taste. Add 250 ml (9 fl oz/1 cup) water and bring to the boil. Reduce the heat, cover and simmer for 20 minutes. Remove the lid, fork through the currants and pine nuts, cover with paper towel, then the lid and leave to cool.

2 Rinse the vine leaves and gently separate. Drain, then dry on paper towel. Trim any thick stems with scissors. Line the base of a 20 cm (8 inch) saucepan with any torn or misshapen leaves. Choose the larger leaves for filling and use the smaller leaves to patch up any gaps.

3 Place a leaf, shiny side down. Spoon a tablespoon of filling into the centre, bring in the sides and roll up tightly from the stem end. Place, seam side down, with the stem end closest to you, in the base of the pan, arranging them close together in a single layer.

4 Pour in the remaining lemon juice, the extra oil and about 185 ml (6 fl oz/¾ cup) water to just cover the dolmades. Cover the dolmades with an inverted plate and place a tin on the plate to firmly compress the dolmades and keep them in place while they are cooking. Cover and bring to the boil, then reduce the heat and simmer for 45 minutes. Cool the dolmades in the pan. Serve at room temperature.

Note Store the dolmades, covered with the cooking liquid, in the refrigerator for up to 2 weeks.

Potato and olive scones

»PREPARATION 25 MINUTES
»COOKING TIME 15 MINUTES »MAKES 15

1 Preheat the oven to 210°C (415°F/ Gas 6–7). Peel and chop 250 g (9 oz) potatoes and boil or microwave until tender. Mash the potatoes with 125 ml (4 fl oz/½ cup) milk. Season with freshly ground black pepper.

2 Pit and chop 3 tablespoons black olives. Sift 250 g (9 oz/2 cups) self-raising flour into a large bowl. Rub in 30 g (1 oz) chopped butter, using your fingertips. Add the olives and 3–4 teaspoons chopped rosemary. and stir until just combined. Make a well in the centre. Add the potato and almost all of 125 ml (4 fl oz/ ½ cup) water. Mix with a flat-bladed knife, using a cutting action, until the mixture forms a soft dough. Add more water if it is too dry.

3 Knead the dough briefly on a lightly floured surface until smooth and press out until 2 cm (¾ inch) thick. Using a floured 5 cm (2 inch) plain round cutter, cut 15 rounds from the dough and place them on a greased baking tray. Brush the tops with milk and cook for about 10–15 minutes until the scones are golden brown.

Grilled tomatoes with bruschetta

»PREPARATION 15 MINUTES »COOKING TIME 15 MINUTES »SERVES 4

1 Preheat a grill (broiler). Halve 4 large ripe tomatoes and gently squeeze out the seeds. Place the tomatoes, cut side down, in a shallow ovenproof dish. Combine ½ teaspoon dried marjoram leaves, 80 ml (2½ fl oz/⅓ cup) olive oil, 2 tablespoons red wine vinegar, 1 teaspoon soft brown sugar, some salt and pepper and mix well. Pour half over the tomatoes.

2 Cook the tomatoes under the hot grill for 30 minutes, turning halfway during cooking. Pour the remaining oil mixture over the tomatoes. Remove the tomatoes from the heat and keep warm.

3 Cut 1 loaf of Italian bread into thick slices. Brush the bread slices liberally with some olive oil, on both sides, and toast until golden. Rub the cut surface of a garlic clove over the bread. Place the cooked tomatoes onto the bread, top with 110 g (3¾ oz/½ cup) chopped, marinated artichokes and sprinkle with 1 tablespoon finely chopped flat-leaf (Italian) parsley and some sea salt.

Lentil and chickpea burgers

»PREPARATION 30 MINUTES »COOKING TIME 30 MINUTES »MAKES 10

250 g (9 oz/1 cup) red lentils
1 tablespoon oil
2 onions, sliced
1 tablespoon tandoori mix powder
425 g (15 oz) tinned chickpeas, drained
1 tablespoon grated fresh ginger
1 egg
3 tablespoons chopped flat-leaf (Italian) parsley
2 tablespoons chopped coriander (cilantro)
180 g (6½ oz/2¼ cups) stale breadcrumbs
plain (all-purpose) flour, to dust

Coriander garlic cream

125 g (4½ oz/½ cup) sour cream
125 ml (4 fl oz/½ cup) cream
1 garlic clove, crushed
2 tablespoons chopped coriander (cilantro)
2 tablespoons chopped flat-leaf (Italian) parsley

1 Prepare and heat a barbecue grill or hotplate. Bring a large saucepan of water to the boil. Add the lentils and simmer for 10 minutes, or until tender. Drain well. Heat the oil in a frying pan and cook the onion until tender. Add the tandoori mix and stir until fragrant. Remove from the heat and cool slightly.

2 Place half the lentils, along with the onion mixture, chickpeas, ginger and egg in a food processor. Process for 20 seconds, or until the mixture is smooth. Transfer to a bowl and stir in the remaining lentils, parsley, coriander and breadcrumbs, and combine well. Divide the mixture into 10 portions.

3 Shape the portions into round patties. (If the mixture is too soft, refrigerate for 15 minutes, to firm.) Toss them in flour and shake off any excess. Place the patties on the lightly greased barbecue. Cook for 3–4 minutes on each side, or until browned, turning once. Serve with the coriander garlic cream.

4 To make the coriander garlic cream, combine the ingredients in a bowl and mix well.

Notes The patties can be prepared up to 2 days ahead and stored in the refrigerator. If you prefer, you can cook the patties in a frying pan brushed lightly with oil.

The coriander garlic cream can be made up to 3 days in advance. Place in a covered container and store in the refrigerator.

Herbed cheese crackers

»PREPARATION 40 MINUTES »COOKING TIME 16 MINUTES »SERVES 4–6

1 Preheat the oven to 190°C (375°F/Gas 5). Line two baking trays with baking paper. Sift the flour and baking powder into a large bowl and add the butter. Rub in the butter with your fingertips until the mixture resembles fine breadcrumbs.

2 Make a well in the centre and add the egg, cheese, herbs and iced water. Mix with a flat-bladed knife, using a cutting action, until the mixture comes together in beads. Gently gather together and lift out onto a lightly floured surface. Press together into a ball.

3 Roll the pastry between sheets of baking paper to 3 mm (⅛ inch) thick. Cut the pastry into rounds, using a 5 cm (2 inch) cutter. Place the rounds onto the baking trays. Re-roll the remaining pastry and repeat the cutting process. Bake for about 8 minutes, or until the biscuits are lightly browned. Transfer to a wire rack to cool.

4 To make the filling, beat the cream cheese and butter in a small bowl using electric beaters until light and creamy. Add the herbs, pepper and cheese and beat until smooth. Spread ½ teaspoon of filling on half of the biscuits and then sandwich together with the remaining biscuits.

Notes You can use chopped lemon thyme instead of parsley.

The biscuits can be made 2 days ahead and stored in an airtight container, or frozen. The filling can be made a day ahead and stored, covered, in the refrigerator.

125 g (4½ oz/1 cup) plain (all-purpose) flour
½ teaspoon baking powder
60 g (2¼ oz) butter, chopped
1 egg, lightly beaten
60 g (2¼ oz) cheddar cheese, grated
1 teaspoon snipped chives
1 teaspoon chopped flat-leaf (Italian) parsley (see Note)
1 tablespoon iced water

Cheese filling

80 g (2¾ oz) cream cheese, softened
20 g (¾ oz) butter
1 tablespoon snipped chives
1 tablespoon chopped flat-leaf (Italian) parsley (see Note)
¼ teaspoon lemon pepper
90 g (3¼ oz) cheddar cheese, grated

Mini onion and parmesan scones

»PREPARATION 25 MINUTES »COOKING TIME 12 MINUTES »MAKES 24

30 g (1 oz) butter
1 small onion, finely chopped
250 g (9 oz/2 cups) self-raising flour, sifted
50 g (1¾ oz/½ cup) finely shredded fresh parmesan cheese
125 ml (4 oz/½ cup) milk
cayenne pepper, to sprinkle

1 Preheat the oven to 210°C (415°F/Gas 6–7). Brush a baking tray with melted butter or oil.

2 Melt the butter in a small frying pan, add the onion and cook, over low heat for 2–3 minutes, or until soft. Cool slightly.

3 Sift the flour and a pinch of salt into a bowl. Stir in the parmesan and make a well in the centre. Add the onion. Combine the milk with 125 ml (4 fl oz/½ cup) water and add almost all of the liquid to the bowl. Mix lightly with a flat-bladed knife, using a cutting action, until the mixture forms a soft dough. Add more liquid if the dough is too dry. Knead briefly on a lightly floured surface until smooth. Press out the dough until 2 cm (¾ inch) thick and cut into 24 rounds with a 3 cm (1¼ inch) plain round cutter. Place the rounds on the prepared tray and lightly sprinkle with the cayenne pepper. Cook the scones for 10–12 minutes, or until they are golden brown.

Note Handle scone dough with a light touch. Cut the liquid in with a knife and take care not to over-knead or your scones will be tough.

Spring rolls

»PREPARATION 45 MINUTES »COOKING TIME 20 MINUTES »MAKES 20

4 dried Chinese mushrooms
150 g (5½ oz) fried tofu
1 large carrot
70 g (2½ oz) water chestnuts
6 spring onions (scallions)
1 tablespoon oil
2 garlic cloves, crushed
1 tablespoon grated fresh ginger
150 g (5½ oz) Chinese cabbage (wong bok), shredded
1 tablespoon soy sauce
white pepper, to taste
sugar, to taste
1 tablespoon cornflour (cornstarch)
10 large spring roll wrappers
oil, extra, for deep-frying

1 Soak the dried mushrooms in boiling water for 20 minutes. Drain and squeeze to remove any excess liquid. Slice the mushroom caps and discard the hard stems.

2 Cut the tofu into fine strips and cut the carrot into very fine batons. Chop the water chestnuts and the spring onions.

3 Heat the oil in a large wok. Swirl to coat the base and side. Stir-fry the garlic, ginger, tofu, carrot and water chestnuts over high heat for 30 seconds. Add the spring onion and Chinese cabbage and cook for 1 minute, or until the cabbage is just softened. Add the soy sauce and some salt, white pepper and sugar, to taste, then allow to cool. Add the sliced mushroom caps.

4 Make a paste by mixing the cornflour with 2 tablespoons water. Cover the spring roll wrappers with a clean damp tea towel (dish towel) while you work. Place two wrappers on a board, one on top of the other. (The rolls are made with two layers of wrappers.) Cut the large square into four squares. Brush the edges of each square with a little cornflour paste. Place 1 tablespoon of filling in the centre of one square. With a corner facing you, firmly roll up the wrapper, folding in the sides as you roll. Repeat with the remaining wrappers and filling.

5 Fill a deep heavy-based saucepan one-third full of oil and heat the oil to 180°C (350°F), or until a cube of bread dropped into the oil browns in 15 seconds. Deep-fry 4 spring rolls at a time for about 3 minutes, or until golden. Drain on crumpled paper towel.

Marinated chilli mushrooms

»PREPARATION 20 MINUTES »COOKING TIME NIL »SERVES 4–6

1 Wipe 750 g (1 lb 10 oz) button mushrooms with damp paper towel to remove any dirt and put them in a bowl.

2 Combine 500 ml (17 fl oz/2 cups) light olive oil, 2 tablespoons lemon juice, 1 finely chopped garlic clove, ¼ teaspoon caster (superfine) sugar and 1 finely chopped green chilli. Pour over the mushrooms and mix until well coated. Cover with plastic wrap and marinate the mushrooms for at least 30 minutes.

3 To serve, add 1 tablespoon chopped coriander (cilantro) and 1 tablespoon chopped flat-leaf (Italian) parsley, then season and mix well.

Parmesan and pesto toasts

»PREPARATION 30 MINUTES
»COOKING TIME 5 MINUTES »SERVES 8–10

1 Freeze 1 baguette until firm. Cut it into very thin slices, using a sharp serrated knife. Toast the slices under a hot grill (broiler) until they are golden brown on both sides.

2 Cut 16 large sun-dried tomatoes into thin strips.

3 To make the pesto, combine 50 g (1¾ oz) basil leaves, 2 tablespoons snipped chives, 50 g (1¾ oz/⅓ cup) pine nuts, 2–3 garlic cloves and 60 ml (2 fl oz/¼ cup) olive oil in a food processor. Process the pesto for 20–30 seconds, or until smooth.

4 Spread the pesto mixture evenly over the toasted baguette slices. Top with strips of sun-dried tomato and thin shavings of parmesan cheese.

Cheese and chive scones

»PREPARATION 20 MINUTES »COOKING TIME 12 MINUTES »MAKES 9

1 Preheat the oven to 210°C (415°F/Gas 6–7). Brush a baking tray with melted butter or oil. Sift the flour and a pinch of salt into a bowl. Rub in the butter using your fingertips. Stir in the cheeses and the chives. Make a well in the centre and add the milk and almost all of 125 ml (4 fl oz/½ cup) water. Mix lightly with a flat-bladed knife to form a soft dough, adding more water if the dough is too dry.

2 Knead the dough briefly on a lightly floured surface until smooth. Press out the dough until it is 2 cm (¾ inch) thick. Using a floured 5 cm (2 inch) plain round cutter, cut nine rounds from the dough. Place the rounds on the prepared baking tray and sprinkle with extra cheese. Bake for 12 minutes, or until the cheese is golden.

250 g (9 oz/2 cups) self-raising flour
30 g (1 oz) butter, chopped
60 g (2¼ oz/½ cup) grated cheddar cheese
3 tablespoons shredded parmesan cheese
2 tablespoons snipped chives
125 ml (4 fl oz/½ cup) milk
3 tablespoons grated cheddar cheese, extra

Grilled vegetables with garlic mayonnaise

»PREPARATION 30 MINUTES »COOKING TIME 14 MINUTES »SERVES 8

1 Sprinkle the eggplant with salt and leave to stand for 30 minutes. Rinse under cold water, then pat dry with paper towel.

2 Halve the leeks and zucchini lengthways. Cut the capsicum in half, remove the seeds and cut each half into four pieces.

3 To make the dressing, combine the vinegar, mustard and oregano in a bowl, then gradually whisk in the oil.

4 Preheat the grill (broiler) to high. Place the eggplant, leek, zucchini and capsicum in a single layer on a flat grill tray, then brush with some of the dressing. Cook under the grill for 5 minutes. Turn the vegetables once, brushing occasionally with the dressing. Add the mushrooms, cap side up, to the grill tray and brush with the dressing. Continue cooking for 10 minutes, or until tender, turning the mushrooms once. Brush the vegetables with the dressing during cooking.

5 To make the mayonnaise, put the egg yolks, lemon juice and garlic in a food processor and process for 5 seconds, or until combined. With the motor running, slowly add the oil in a thin, steady stream until it is all added and the mayonnaise is thick and creamy. Add the chives, parsley and 1 tablespoon water and blend for 3 seconds until combined. Serve with the grilled vegetables.

Note The garlic mayonnaise can be made several days ahead and refrigerated. Do not worry if the dressing separates — simply brush on as required.

2 eggplants (aubergines), thinly sliced
4 small leeks, white part only
4 small zucchini (courgettes)
2 red capsicums (peppers)
8 large flat mushrooms

Dressing

1 tablespoon balsamic vinegar
2 tablespoons dijon mustard
2 teaspoons dried oregano leaves
250 ml (9 fl oz/1 cup) olive oil

Garlic mayonnaise

2 egg yolks
1 tablespoon lemon juice
2 garlic cloves, crushed
250 ml (9 fl oz/1 cup) olive oil
1 tablespoon snipped chives
1 tablespoon chopped flat-leaf (Italian) parsley

Nachos with guacamole

»PREPARATION 20 MINUTES »COOKING TIME 5 MINUTES »SERVES 4–6

1 To make the guacamole, finely chop the spring onion and tomato. Cut the avocado in half, peel and discard the stone. Mash the flesh lightly with a fork. Combine the avocado with the spring onion, tomato, lemon juice and some freshly ground black pepper.

2 Preheat the oven to 180°C (350°F/Gas 4). Combine the beans and salsa, then divide the mixture among four ovenproof serving plates. Cover with the corn chips and grated cheese. Put in the oven for 3–5 minutes, or until the cheese has melted.

3 Spoon the extra salsa onto the melted cheese, then top with some of the guacamole and sour cream.

Guacamole

1 spring onion (scallion)
1 small tomato
1 large avocado
1 tablespoon lemon juice

440 g (15½ oz) tinned red kidney beans, rinsed and drained
90 g (3¼ oz/⅓ cup) ready-made tomato salsa
250 g (9 oz) corn chips
250 g (9 oz/2 cups) grated cheddar cheese
375 g (13 oz/1½ cups) ready-made tomato salsa, extra
90 g (3¼ oz/⅓ cup) sour cream

Capsicum and corn muffins

»PREPARATION 15 MINUTES »COOKING TIME 20 MINUTES »MAKES 15

1 Preheat the oven to 210°C (415°F/Gas 6–7). Brush a 12-hole muffin tin with oil or melted butter. Sift the flour, baking powder and ¼ teaspoon salt into a large bowl. Add the polenta and sugar. Stir until thoroughly combined. Make a well in the centre.

2 Combine the egg, milk, Tabasco and oil in a separate bowl. Add the egg mixture, capsicum, corn and parsley all at once to the dry ingredients. Stir quickly with a wooden spoon or rubber spatula until all the ingredients are just moistened. (Do not over-mix — the batter should be quite lumpy.)

3 Spoon the mixture into the tin and bake for 20 minutes, or until golden. Loosen with a knife but leave in the tin for 2 minutes. Cool the muffins on a wire rack.

- 125 g (4½ oz/1 cup) plain (all-purpose) flour
- 1 tablespoon baking powder
- 150 g (5½ oz/1 cup) fine polenta
- 1 tablespoon caster (superfine) sugar
- 1 egg
- 170 ml (5½ fl oz/⅔ cup) milk
- ¼ teaspoon Tabasco sauce (optional)
- 60 ml (2 fl oz/¼ cup) oil
- ½ red capsicum (pepper), seeded and finely chopped
- 440 g (15½ oz) tinned corn kernels, drained
- 3 tablespoons finely chopped flat-leaf (Italian) parsley

Potato and herb fritters

»PREPARATION 25 MINUTES
»COOKING TIME 8 MINUTES »SERVES 4–6

1 Finely grate 620 g (1 lb 6 oz) potato and 185 g (6½ oz) orange sweet potato and put in a bowl. Add 30 g (1 oz/¼ cup) sifted plain (all-purpose) flour, 3 tablespoons finely snipped chives, 2 tablespoons finely chopped flat-leaf (Italian) parsley, 1 tablespoon finely chopped oregano and 2 lightly beaten eggs. Stir with a wooden spoon until all the ingredients are just combined.

2 Heat 1 tablespoon olive oil in a heavy-based frying pan. Spoon heaped tablespoons of the mixture into the pan. Cook over medium–high heat for 4 minutes each side, or until golden. Serve the fritters warm, topped with some light sour cream and dill sprigs.

Spicy fried chickpeas

»PREPARATION 30 MINUTES
»COOKING TIME 15 MINUTES »SERVES 6–8

1 Put 300 g (10½ oz) of dried chickpeas in a large bowl, cover with plenty of cold water and soak overnight. Drain well and pat dry with paper towel.

2 Fill a deep heavy-based saucepan one-third full of oil. Heat to 180°C (350°F), or until a cube of bread dropped into the oil browns in 15 seconds. Deep-fry half of the chickpeas for 3 minutes. Remove with a slotted spoon. Drain on crumpled paper towel and repeat with the rest of the chickpeas. Partially cover the pan as some chickpeas may pop. Do not leave the oil unattended.

3 Reheat the oil. Fry the chickpeas again in batches for 3 minutes each batch, or until browned. Drain.

4 Combine ½ teaspoon mild or hot paprika with ¼ teaspoon cayenne pepper and some salt, and sprinkle over the hot chickpeas. Leave to cool, then serve.

Avocado with lime and chillies

»PREPARATION 20 MINUTES
»COOKING TIME NIL »SERVES 6

1 Combine 1 teaspoon finely grated lime zest, 2 tablespoons lime juice, 1 teaspoon soft brown sugar, 1 tablespoon olive oil, 1 tablespoon chopped flat-leaf (Italian) parsley and 2–3 seeded and diced jalapeño chillies in a small bowl.

2 Slice 2 ripe avocados and put on a serving plate. Pour the lime and chilli over the avocado and serve.

Note The lime juice prevents the avocados from browning. Lemon juice may be substituted.

Baked ricotta

»PREPARATION 15 MINUTES
»COOKING TIME 30 MINUTES »SERVES 8–10

1 Remove any paper from the base of 2 kg (4 lb 8 oz) whole ricotta cheese. Put the ricotta in a plastic colander and place over a bowl, ensuring the base of the colander is not touching the base of the bowl. Cover with plastic wrap and leave to drain overnight in the refrigerator.

2 Preheat the oven to 250°C (500°F/Gas 9) and line a baking tray with baking paper. Put the ricotta on the tray and brush with a little olive oil. Bake for 30 minutes, or until the ricotta is golden brown. Allow to cool slightly.

3 Mix 170 ml (5½ fl oz/⅔ cup) of olive oil with 185 ml (6 fl oz/¾ cup) lemon juice, 2 tablespoons strips of lemon zest, 2 crushed garlic cloves and 25 g (1 oz) finely shredded basil in a bowl and season to taste.

4 Roughly chop 50 g (2 oz/⅓ cup) semi-dried (sun-blushed) tomatoes. Place the whole ricotta on a platter, pour on the dressing and scatter with the semi-dried tomatoes. Serve with thin slices of Italian-style bread or bruschetta.

Zucchini and carrot muffins

»PREPARATION 20 MINUTES »COOKING TIME 20 MINUTES »MAKES 12

1 Preheat the oven to 210°C (415°F/Gas 6–7). Brush a 12-hole muffin tin with melted butter or oil. Grate 2 zucchini (courgettes) and 2 carrots. Sift 250 g (9 oz/2 cups) of self-raising flour, 1 teaspoon ground cinnamon, ½ teaspoon freshly grated nutmeg and a pinch of salt into a large bowl. Add the carrot, zucchini and 60 g (2¼ oz/½ cup) chopped pecans. Stir until all the ingredients are well combined.

2 Combine 2 eggs, 250 ml (9 fl oz/ 1 cup) milk and 90 g (3¼ oz) melted butter in a separate bowl and whisk well until combined.

3 Make a well in the centre of the flour mixture and add the egg mixture all at once. Mix quickly with a fork or spatula until the ingredients are just moistened. (Do not over-mix — the batter should be quite lumpy.)

4 Spoon the batter into the tin. Bake for 15–20 minutes, or until golden. Loosen the muffins with a flat-bladed knife or spatula and leave in the tin for 2 minutes, then turn out onto a wire rack to cool.

38 Okra with tomato sauce

34 Mediterranean lentil salad

41 Orange and date salad

43 **Lentil and silverbeet soup**

54 **Green papaya salad**

Salads, side dishes and soups

Warm lentil and rice salad

»PREPARATION 15 MINUTES »COOKING TIME 40 MINUTES »SERVES 6

1 Cook the lentils and basmati rice in separate saucepans of water until they are just tender, then drain.

2 Meanwhile, cook the onion and garlic in the oil and butter over low heat for 30 minutes, until very soft.

3 Stir in the cinnamon, paprika, cumin and coriander and cook for a few minutes longer.

4 Combine the onion and spice mixture with the well-drained rice and lentils. Stir in the chopped spring onions until combined, then add freshly ground black pepper to taste. Serve warm.

Note Do not use red lentils for this recipe as they become mushy and do not retain their shape. It is not necessary to soak the lentils, but they need to be rinsed thoroughly.

185 g (6½ oz/1 cup) green lentils (see Note)
200 g (7 oz/1 cup) basmati rice
4 large red onions, thinly sliced
4 garlic cloves, crushed
250 ml (9 fl oz/1 cup) olive oil
45 g (1¾ oz) butter
2 teaspoons ground cinnamon
2 teaspoons ground sweet paprika
2 teaspoons ground cumin
2 teaspoons ground coriander
3 spring onions (scallions), chopped

Sprout and pear salad with sesame dressing

»PREPARATION 30 MINUTES »COOKING TIME NIL »SERVES 6

1 Rinse and drain the snow pea sprouts. Remove the brown tips from the bean sprouts. Snip the chives into 4 cm (1½ inch) lengths and cut the snow peas and celery into thin matchstick strips.

2 Peel and core the pears, then slice into thin strips, slightly wider than the celery and the snow peas. Place in a bowl and cover with water to prevent discoloration.

3 To make the sesame dressing, combine all of the ingredients and mix thoroughly.

4 Drain the pears. Combine all the salad ingredients and the coriander sprigs in a large serving bowl. Pour the dressing over and toss lightly.

5 Sprinkle with sesame seeds and serve immediately.

250 g (9 oz) snow pea (mangetout) sprouts
250 g (9 oz) bean sprouts
30 g (1 oz) chives
100 g (3½ oz) snow peas (mangetout)
1 celery stalk
2 firm pears (not green)
coriander (cilantro) sprigs
sesame seeds, to garnish

Sesame dressing
2 tablespoons soy sauce
1 teaspoon sesame oil
1 tablespoon soft brown sugar
2 tablespoons peanut oil
1 tablespoon rice vinegar

Ratatouille

»PREPARATION 25 MINUTES »COOKING TIME 40 MINUTES »SERVES 4–6

1 Score a cross in the base of each tomato. Put in a heatproof bowl and cover with boiling water. Leave for 30 seconds, then transfer to cold water, drain and peel away the skin from the cross. Cut the tomatoes in half, scoop out the seeds and chop the flesh.

2 Cut the eggplants and zucchini into 2 cm (¾ inch) cubes. Cut the green capsicum in half, remove the seeds and membrane and cut into 2 cm (¾ inch) squares. Cut the red onion into 2 cm (¾ inch) wedges.

3 Heat 2 tablespoons of the oil in a large saucepan, add the eggplant and cook over medium heat for 4–5 minutes, or until softened but not browned. Remove the eggplant from the pan and add another 2 tablespoons oil to the pan. Cook the zucchini for 3–4 minutes, or until softened. Remove. Add the green capsicum, cook for 2 minutes and remove.

4 Heat the remaining oil, add the onion and cook for 2–3 minutes, or until softened. Add the garlic, cayenne pepper, thyme and the bay leaves. Cook, stirring, for 1 minute.

5 Return the eggplant, zucchini and capsicum to the pan. Add the tomato, vinegar and sugar. Simmer for 20 minutes, stirring occasionally. Stir in the basil and season. Serve hot or at room temperature.

Note You can also serve ratatouille as a starter with bread.

6 vine-ripened tomatoes
500 g (1 lb 2 oz) eggplants (aubergines)
375 g (13 oz) zucchini (courgettes)
1 green capsicum (pepper)
1 red onion
100 ml (3½ fl oz) olive oil
3 garlic cloves, finely chopped
¼ teaspoon cayenne pepper
2 teaspoons chopped thyme
2 bay leaves
1 tablespoon red wine vinegar
1 teaspoon caster (superfine) sugar
3 tablespoons shredded basil

Mediterranean lentil salad

»PREPARATION 20 MINUTES »COOKING TIME 20 MINUTES »SERVES 4–6

1 Halve the capsicums lengthways. Remove the seeds and membrane and then cut them into large, flattish pieces. Grill (broil) the capsicum until the skin blackens and blisters. Put the capsicum on a chopping board, cover with a tea towel (dish towel) and leave to cool. Peel the capsicum and cut the flesh into 5 mm (¼ inch) strips.

2 Cook the lentils in boiling water for 10 minutes, or until tender (do not overcook, as they will become mushy). Drain well. Put the lentils, capsicum, onion and cucumber in a bowl and toss to combine.

3 To make the dressing, put the olive oil, lemon juice, cumin, garlic and some salt and pepper into a small bowl and whisk to combine.

4 Pour the dressing over the salad and mix well. Cover the salad and refrigerate for 4 hours. Bring the salad back to room temperature before serving.

1 large red capsicum (pepper)
1 large yellow capsicum (pepper)
250 g (9 oz/1 cup) red lentils
1 red onion, finely chopped
1 Lebanese (short) cucumber, chopped

Dressing

80 ml (2½ fl oz/⅓ cup) olive oil
2 tablespoons lemon juice
1 teaspoon ground cumin
2 garlic cloves, crushed

Snow pea salad

»PREPARATION 25 MINUTES »COOKING TIME 5 MINUTES »SERVES 4–6

1 Slice the snow peas diagonally. Cut the capsicum in half, remove the seeds and membrane and slice.

2 Combine the snow peas, red capsicum, lettuces, tomatoes and watercress in a large bowl.

3 To make the croutons, remove the crusts from the bread and discard the crusts. Cut the bread into 1 cm (½ inch) squares. Heat the olive oil in a small, heavy-based frying pan and add the crushed garlic. Stir in the bread cubes and cook until golden and crisp. Remove from the heat and leave to drain well on paper towel.

4 To make the dressing, whisk all the ingredients together with some cracked black pepper in a small bowl until combined.

5 Just before serving, top the salad with the croutons and parmesan shavings. Drizzle with the dressing.

200 g (7 oz) snow peas (mangetout)
1 large red capsicum (pepper)
4 leaves oak leaf lettuce
5 leaves green coral lettuce
250 g (9 oz) cherry tomatoes
60 g (2¼ oz) watercress sprigs
parmesan cheese shavings, to serve

Garlic croutons

3 slices white bread
60 ml (2 fl oz/¼ cup) olive oil
1 garlic clove, crushed

Dressing

2 tablespoons olive oil
1 tablespoon mayonnaise
1 tablespoon sour cream
2 tablespoons lemon juice
1 teaspoon soft brown sugar

Cooked vegetable salad

»PREPARATION 45 MINUTES »COOKING TIME 15 MINUTES »SERVES 4

1 Cut the turnip into thin strips. Slice the onion into thin rings. Slice the celery stalks and mushrooms. Cut the carrot into fine strips. Cut the capsicum in half, remove the seeds and membrane and cut into fine strips. Chop the spring onions.

2 Put the turnip on a plate lined with paper towel. Sprinkle with 2 teaspoons salt and set aside for at least 20 minutes. Rinse the turnip under cold water and pat dry with paper towel.

3 Heat the combined oils in a large frying pan or wok and swirl to coat the base and side. Stir-fry the turnip, garlic and onion over medium heat for 3 minutes, or until lightly golden.

4 Add the celery, mushrooms, carrot, red capsicum and spring onion and toss well. Cover and steam for 1 minute. Remove the vegetables from the wok and set aside to cool.

5 To make the dressing, combine all the ingredients in a bowl. Pour the dressing over the vegetables and toss to combine. Arrange on a serving plate and sprinkle with the pine nuts.

Note Toast the pine nuts in a dry frying pan over medium heat, stirring constantly, until they are golden brown and fragrant. Watch carefully as they will burn easily.

1 small turnip
1 large onion
2 celery stalks
200 g (7 oz) button mushrooms
1 large carrot
½ red capsicum (pepper)
4 spring onions (scallions)
2 tablespoons sesame oil
1 tablespoon oil
2 garlic cloves, finely chopped
80 g (2¾ oz/½ cup) pine nuts, toasted (see Note)

Dressing

60 ml (2 fl oz/¼ cup) soy sauce
1 tablespoon white vinegar
3 cm (1¼ inch) piece fresh ginger, very finely sliced and cut into fine strips
1–2 teaspoons soft brown sugar

Pomegranate and olive salad

»PREPARATION 10 MINUTES
»COOKING TIME 5 MINUTES »SERVES 4

1 Soak 100 g (3½ oz/1 cup) of walnut halves in boiling water for 3–4 minutes, or until the skins peel off readily. Drain, peel and pat dry. Lightly toast the walnuts under a medium grill (broiler), then cool and roughly chop.

2 Put 125 ml (4 fl oz/½ cup) olive oil, 1½ tablespoons pomegranate syrup and ½ teaspoon chilli flakes in a small bowl and mix thoroughly.

3 Pit and halve 350 g (12 oz/2 cups) green olives. Put the olives, 175 g (6 oz/1 cup) pomegranate seeds, 1 chopped large red onion, 20 g (¾ oz) flat-leaf (Italian) parsley leaves and the walnuts in a bowl and toss. Just before serving, pour over the dressing, season to taste, and combine well.

Chickpea and olive salad

»PREPARATION 20 MINUTES
»COOKING TIME 25 MINUTES »SERVES 6

1 Place 330 g (11¾ oz/1½ cups) dried chickpeas in a large bowl and cover with cold water. Leave to soak overnight. Drain the chickpeas, put in a saucepan and cover with fresh water. Cook for 25 minutes, or until just tender. Drain and cool.

2 Cut 1 small Lebanese (short) cucumber in half lengthways, scoop out the seeds and thickly slices. Cut 2 tomatoes into cubes the same size as the chickpeas. Put the cucumber and tomato in a serving bowl with 1 finely chopped small red onion, 60 g (2¼ oz/½ cup) pitted black olives, 3 tablespoons chopped of flat-leaf (Italian) parsley, and the cooled chickpeas.

3 Combine 60 ml (2 fl oz/¼ cup) olive oil, 1 tablespoon lemon juice, 1 teaspoon honey and 1 crushed garlic clove. Pour over the salad and lightly toss to combine. Serve at room temperature.

Spicy tofu and vegetable salad

»PREPARATION 20 MINUTES
»COOKING TIME NIL »SERVES 4

1 Cut 250 g (9 oz) firm tofu into 2 cm (¾ inch) cubes and place in a bowl. Combine ½ teaspoon grated fresh ginger, 1 crushed garlic clove, 2 teaspoons soy sauce, 2 teaspoons sweet chilli sauce and 2 tablespoons oil. Pour over the tofu and gently stir. Cover with plastic wrap and refrigerate for 1 hour.

2 Slice 100 g (3½ oz) snow peas (mangetout) into 3 cm (1¼ inch) lengths. Place in a small saucepan, cover with boiling water and leave to stand for 1 minute, then drain and transfer to iced water to stop the cooking process. Drain well.

3 Cut 2 small carrots into batons, and finely shred 100 g (3½ oz) red cabbage. Add the snow pea pieces, carrots and cabbage to the tofu and toss lightly to combine. Transfer to a serving bowl or individual plates, then sprinkle with 2 tablespoons chopped peanuts and serve.

Okra with tomato sauce

»PREPARATION 5 MINUTES »COOKING TIME 15 MINUTES »SERVES 4–6

1 Heat 60 ml (2 fl oz/¼ cup) olive oil in a large frying pan and cook 1 chopped onion over medium heat for 5 minutes, or until transparent and golden. Add 2 crushed garlic cloves and cook for another minute.

2 Add 500 g (1 lb 2 oz) fresh okra to the frying pan and cook, stirring, for 4–5 minutes. Add 400 g (14 oz) tinned chopped tomatoes, 60 ml (2 fl oz/¼ cup) lemon juice and 2 teaspoons sugar. Simmer, stirring occasionally, for 3–4 minutes, or until softened. Stir in 60 g (2¼ oz) finely chopped coriander (cilantro), remove from the heat and serve.

Note If fresh okra is not available, you can use 800 g (1 lb 12 oz) of tinned okra instead. Rinse and drain the okra before adding with the coriander.

Tunisian carrot salad

»PREPARATION 10 MINUTES »COOKING TIME 10 MINUTES »SERVES 6–8

1 Thinly slice 500 g (1 lb 2 oz) carrots. Put 500 ml (17 fl oz/2 cups) water in a saucepan and bring to the boil. Add the carrot and cook until tender. Drain and put in a bowl.

2 Add 3 tablespoons finely chopped flat-leaf (Italian) parsley, 2 crushed garlic cloves, 1 teaspoon ground cumin, 80 ml (2½ fl oz/⅓ cup) olive oil and 60 ml (2 fl oz/¼ cup) red wine vinegar to the carrot. Season with ¼–½ teaspoon ready-made harissa and some salt and pepper. Stir well.

3 Put the carrot in a serving dish and garnish with 12 black olives and 2 quartered hard-boiled eggs.

Note If the carrots are not sweet, add a little honey to the dressing. Harissa is a spicy paste blend available from delicatessens.

Grilled vegetable salad

»PREPARATION 15 MINUTES »COOKING TIME 10 MINUTES »SERVES 4

1 Without slicing through the base, cut the onion from top to base into six sections, leaving it attached at the base.

2 Put the onion on a barbecue, or over an open-flamed grill or gas stovetop, with the eggplants and capsicums. Cook the vegetables over moderate heat for 10 minutes, turning them occasionally, until the eggplants and capsicum skins are blackened and blistered. Cool the capsicums in a plastic bag for 10 minutes and set the onion and eggplant aside.

3 Dry-fry the capers with a pinch of salt until crisp.

4 Cut the onion into its six sections and discard the charred outer skins. Peel the skins off the eggplants and remove the stalk. Slice from top to bottom. Peel the capsicums, cut in half and remove the seeds and membrane. Cut into thick slices.

5 Arrange all the vegetables on a large platter. Drizzle the olive oil over them and season. Scatter the parsley, garlic and fried capers over the top. Serve cold.

Note Grilling the vegetables under a griller (broiler) or roasting them in a hot oven also works, although the dish will lack the characteristic smoky flavour.

1 red onion
6 small eggplants (aubergines), about 16 cm (6¼ inches) long
4 red capsicums (peppers)
4 orange capsicums (peppers)
1 tablespoon baby capers
80 ml (2½ fl oz/⅓ cup) good-quality olive oil
1 tablespoon chopped flat-leaf (Italian) parsley
2 garlic cloves, finely chopped

Fast pasta soup

»PREPARATION 20 MINUTES »COOKING TIME 35 MINUTES »SERVES 4

1 Heat the oil in a saucepan over medium heat. Stir-fry the spring onion, snow peas and mushrooms for about 3 minutes, or until they are just tender.

2 Add the garlic and ginger and stir for 1 minute. Pour in the stock and bring to the boil. Once boiling, add the pasta and cook for 3 minutes, or until just tender. Serve immediately.

1 tablespoon oil
2 spring onions (scallions), chopped
150 g (5½ oz) snow peas (mangetout), trimmed and cut into pieces
200 g (7 oz) mushrooms, sliced
2 garlic cloves, crushed
1 teaspoon grated fresh ginger
1 litre (35 fl oz/4 cups) vegetable stock
150 g (5½ oz) angel hair pasta

Orange and date salad

»PREPARATION 30 MINUTES »COOKING TIME NIL »SERVES 4–6

6 navel oranges
2 teaspoons orange blossom water
8 dates, pitted and thinly sliced lengthways
90 g (3 1/4 oz/3/4 cup) slivered almonds, lightly toasted (see Notes)
1 tablespoon shredded mint
1/4 teaspoon ras el hanout (see Notes) or ground cinnamon

1 Peel the oranges, removing all the pith. Section them by cutting away all the membrane from the flesh. Place the orange segments in a bowl and squeeze the juice from the remainder of the oranges over them. Add the orange blossom water and stir gently to combine. Cover and refrigerate until chilled.

2 Place the orange segments and juice on a large flat serving dish and scatter the dates and almonds over the top. Sprinkle the mint and ras el hanout over the orange segments. Serve chilled.

Notes Toast the almonds in a dry frying pan over medium heat, stirring constantly, until they are lightly golden. Watch carefully as they will burn easily.

Ras el hanout is a spice mixture used in Moroccan cooking.

Pumpkin with chilli and avocado

»PREPARATION 20 MINUTES »COOKING TIME 10 MINUTES »SERVES 6

1 Scrape the seeds from the inside of the pumpkin. Cut the pumpkin into slices and remove the skin. Cook the pumpkin in a saucepan of simmering water until tender but still firm. Remove from the heat and drain well.

2 To make the dressing, combine all the ingredients in a small bowl.

3 Cut the avocado in half and remove the stone. Peel the avocado, then cut the flesh into thin slices.

4 Combine the warm pumpkin and avocado in a serving bowl. Gently toss the coriander dressing through. Serve immediately.

Notes Assemble this dish just before serving. The dressing can be made up several hours in advance. Store, covered, in the refrigerator.

Add one small, finely chopped red chilli to the dressing if you want a spicier flavour.

750 g (1 lb 10 oz) pumpkin (winter squash)
1 large avocado

Dressing

1 small red onion, finely chopped
2 tablespoons olive oil
1 tablespoon chopped coriander (cilantro) leaves
1 tablespoon chopped mint
2 teaspoons sweet chilli sauce
2 teaspoons balsamic vinegar
1 teaspoon soft brown sugar

Lentil and silverbeet soup

»PREPARATION 20 MINUTES »COOKING TIME 1 HOUR 20 MINUTES »SERVES 6

1 Put the lentils in a large saucepan with the vegetable stock and 1 litre (35 fl oz/4 cups) water. Bring to the boil, then reduce the heat. Simmer, covered, for 1 hour.

2 Meanwhile, remove the stems from the silverbeet and shred the leaves. Heat the oil in a saucepan over medium heat and cook the onion for 2–3 minutes, or until transparent. Add the crushed garlic and cook for 1 minute. Add the silverbeet and toss for 2–3 minutes, or until wilted.

3 Stir the silverbeet mixture into the lentils. Add the coriander and lemon juice, season, and simmer, covered, for 15–20 minutes. Serve with the lemon wedges.

280 g (10 oz/1 1/2 cups) brown lentils, rinsed and drained
1 litre (35 fl oz/4 cups) vegetable stock
850 g (1 lb 14 oz) silverbeet (Swiss chard)
60 ml (2 fl oz/1/4 cup) olive oil
1 large onion, finely chopped
4 garlic cloves, crushed
35 g (1 1/4 oz) finely chopped coriander (cilantro) leaves
80 ml (2 1/2 fl oz/1/3 cup) lemon juice
lemon wedges, to serve

Sweet potato rosti

»PREPARATION 30 MINUTES »COOKING TIME 45 MINUTES »MAKES 30

3 orange sweet potatoes, unpeeled
2 teaspoons cornflour (cornstarch)
40 g (1 ½ oz) butter
150 g (5½ oz) mozzarella cheese, cut into 30 cubes

1 Boil or microwave the orange sweet potatoes until almost cooked, but still firm. Set aside to cool, then peel and roughly grate into a bowl. Add the cornflour and ½ teaspoon salt and toss lightly to combine.

2 Melt a little of the butter in a frying pan. Spoon teaspoons of the potato in the pan and put a cube of cheese in the centre of each mound. Top with another teaspoon of the potato and gently flatten to form rough circles. Increase the heat to medium and cook for 3 minutes each side, or until golden. Repeat with the remaining potato mixture and mozzarella cubes.

Note The sweet potato can be cooked and grated up to 2 hours ahead and set aside, covered, until serving time. Assemble and cook the rosti close to serving time.

Baked vegetables with ginger glaze

»PREPARATION 25 MINUTES »COOKING TIME 1 HOUR 10 MINUTES »SERVES 4

1 Preheat the oven to 210°C (415°F/Gas 6–7) and brush a large baking tray with oil. Cut the sweet potato, potato, carrot, parsnip and turnip into sticks 5 cm (2 inches) long and 1 cm (½ inch) thick.

2 Place the vegetables in a single layer on the prepared baking tray and brush them all over with olive oil. Bake for 1 hour, or until golden.

3 Melt the butter in a small saucepan. Add the sugar and stir over low heat until the sugar has dissolved. Add the grated ginger and 60 ml (2 fl oz/¼ cup) water and stir to combine. Bring to the boil, then reduce the heat and simmer, for 5 minutes, or until the mixture has reduced and thickened slightly. Pour the glaze over the vegetables, toss to coat and return the tray to the oven for 5 minutes. Serve immediately.

150 g (5½ oz) orange sweet potato
1 potato
1 carrot
1 parsnip
1 turnip
2 tablespoons olive oil
60 g (2¼ oz) butter
2 tablespoons caster (superfine) sugar
1 tablespoon finely grated fresh ginger

Spinach with raisins and pine nuts

»PREPARATION 15 MINUTES »COOKING TIME 15 MINUTES »SERVES 6

1 Trim the stalks from the spinach and discard. Wash and shred the leaves. Slice the onion.

2 Put the pine nuts in a frying pan and stir over medium heat for 3 minutes, or until lightly brown. Remove from the pan.

3 Heat the oil in the same pan, add the onion and cook over low heat, stirring occasionally, for 10 minutes, or until translucent. Increase the heat to medium, add the garlic and cook for 1 minute. Add the spinach with the water clinging to it, the raisins and cinnamon. Cover and cook for 2 minutes, or until the spinach wilts. Stir in the pine nuts, and season to taste.

Note Silverbeet (Swiss chard) works equally well in this recipe, although it may take longer to cook than spinach.

500 g (1 lb 2 oz) English spinach
1 small red onion
2 tablespoons pine nuts
1 tablespoon olive oil
1 garlic clove, thinly sliced
2 tablespoons raisins
pinch ground cinnamon

Ratatouille and pasta soup

»PREPARATION 25 MINUTES »COOKING TIME 40 MINUTES »SERVES 6

1 Spread the eggplant pieces out in a colander and sprinkle generously with salt. Set aside for 20 minutes, then rinse thoroughly. Pat dry with paper towels.

2 Heat the oil in a large heavy-based saucepan and cook the onion over medium heat for 10 minutes, or until soft and lightly golden. Add the capsicums, garlic, zucchini and eggplant and stir-fry for 5 minutes.

3 Add the tomatoes, herbs and vegetable stock. Bring to the boil, then reduce the heat and simmer for 10 minutes, until the vegetables are tender. Add the fusilli and cook for a further 15 minutes, or until the fusilli is tender. Serve with shavings of parmesan scattered on top.

1 eggplant (aubergine), chopped
2 tablespoons olive oil
1 large onion, chopped
1 large red capsicum (pepper), chopped
1 large green capsicum (pepper), chopped
2 garlic cloves, crushed
3 zucchini (courgettes), sliced
800 g (1 lb 12 oz) tinned crushed tomatoes
1 teaspoon dried oregano leaves
½ teaspoon dried thyme leaves
1 litre (35 fl oz/4 cups) vegetable stock
50 g (1¾ oz) fusilli
fresh parmesan cheese shavings, to serve

Green pea soup

»PREPARATION 20 MINUTES »COOKING TIME 1 HOUR 40 MINUTES »SERVES 4

1 Soak the split peas in cold water for 2 hours, then drain well.

2 Heat the oil in a large heavy-based saucepan. Add the onion, celery and carrot and cook over medium heat for 3 minutes, stirring occasionally, until soft but not browned. Stir in the cumin, coriander and ginger, then cook for 1 minute. Add the split peas and stock to the pan. Bring to the boil, then reduce the heat to low and simmer, covered, for 1½ hours, stirring occasionally. Add the frozen peas to the pan and stir to combine.

3 Allow the soup to cool slightly before transferring to a food processor. Blend, in batches, until smooth. Return to a clean pan and gently reheat. Season to taste and then stir in the chopped mint. Serve in bowls with a swirl of yoghurt or sour cream.

335 g (11¾ oz/1½ cups) dried green split peas
2 tablespoons oil
1 onion, finely chopped
1 celery stalk, finely sliced
1 carrot, finely sliced
1 tablespoon ground cumin
1 tablespoon ground coriander
2 teaspoons grated fresh ginger
1.25 litres (44 fl oz/5 cups) vegetable stock
310 g (11 oz/2 cups) frozen green peas
1 tablespoon chopped mint
yoghurt or sour cream, to serve

Creamy corn and tomato soup

»PREPARATION 20 MINUTES »COOKING TIME 15 MINUTES »SERVES 4–6

1 Heat the oil in a large saucepan. Add the stock powder and onion and cook until the onion is soft.

2 Score a cross in the base of the tomatoes. Put in a heatproof bowl and cover with boiling water. Leave for 30 seconds, then transfer to a bowl of cold water and peel the skin away from the cross. Cut the tomato in half, scoop out the seeds and chop the flesh.

3 Add the tomato to the pan with the tomato paste, creamed corn and corn kernels. Season with the chilli and stir until heated through. Serve with a dollop of sour cream and some warm tortillas.

1 teaspoon olive oil
1 teaspoon vegetable stock (bouillon) powder
1 onion, finely chopped
3 tomatoes
425 g (15 oz) tomato paste (concentrated purée)
310 g (11 oz) tinned creamed corn
125 g (4½ oz) tinned corn kernels, drained
chilli powder, to taste
sour cream and tortillas, to serve

Eggplant salad

»PREPARATION 20 MINUTES »COOKING TIME 1 HOUR 35 MINUTES »SERVES 6

1 Cut the eggplants into 2 cm (¾ inch) cubes. Put in a colander and sprinkle generously with salt. Leave for 30 minutes, rinse under cold water, then pat dry with a tea towel (dish towel).

2 Heat 2 tablespoons of the oil in a large frying pan and fry batches of eggplant until golden, adding more oil if necessary. Drain on paper towels.

3 Heat another 2 tablespoons of the oil in the pan. and fry the onion for 1 minute. Add the cinnamon and half the garlic and cook for 1 minute, then add the tomato. Add the eggplant and simmer for 1 hour, or until the mixture is quite dry. Add half of each of the parsley and coriander. Stir and leave to cool.

4 Mix 2 tablespoons of oil with the lemon juice and add the remaining crushed garlic and the mint. Stir into the yoghurt.

5 Toss the pine nuts through the eggplant salad and garnish with the remaining herbs. Serve at room temperature with the dressing.

1 kg (2 lb 4 oz) large eggplants (aubergines)

125 ml (4 fl oz/½ cup) olive oil

1 onion, finely chopped

½ teaspoon ground cinnamon

4 garlic cloves, crushed

800 g (1 lb 12 oz) tinned crushed tomatoes

3 tablespoons chopped flat-leaf (Italian) parsley

2 tablespoons chopped coriander (cilantro) leaves

1 tablespoon lemon juice

2 tablespoons chopped mint

150 g (5½ oz) Greek-style yoghurt

25 g (1 oz) pine nuts, toasted

Fast melon salad

»PREPARATION 15 MINUTES
»COOKING TIME NIL »SERVES 4–6

1 Cut a large honeydew melon into thin slices and arrange on a large platter. Scatter 60 g (2¼ oz/2 cups) watercress sprigs over the top. Top with 2 sliced avocados and 1 thinly sliced red capsicum. Scatter 220 g (7¾ oz) crumbled marinated feta cheese and 90 g (3¼ oz) niçoise olives on top.

2 To make the dressing, put 60 ml (2 fl oz/¼ cup) olive oil, 2 tablespoons white wine vinegar and 1 teaspoon dijon mustard in a screw-top jar and shake until combined. Drizzle the dressing over the salad.

Red capsicum soup

»PREPARATION 20 MINUTES »COOKING TIME 30 MINUTES »SERVES 6

1 Cut the capsicums into quarters. Remove the seeds and membrane. Grill (broil) until the skin blackens and blisters. Place on a chopping board and cover with a tea towel (dish towel). Cool before peeling and chopping.

2 Score a cross in the base of the tomatoes. Put in a heatproof bowl and cover with boiling water. Leave for 30 seconds, then transfer to cold water and peel the skin away from the cross. Cut the tomatoes in half, scoop out the seeds and roughly chop the flesh.

3 Heat the oil in a large saucepan. Add the marjoram, mixed herbs, garlic and curry paste. Stir over low heat for 1 minute, or until aromatic. Add the onion and leek and cook for 3 minutes or until golden. Add the cabbage, capsicum, tomato and 1 litre (35 fl oz/4 cups) water. Bring to the boil, then reduce the heat and simmer for 20 minutes. Remove the pan from the heat and cool slightly.

4 Transfer the soup to a food processor and blend, in batches, for 30 seconds, or until smooth. Return the soup to a clean saucepan, stir through the chilli sauce and season with salt and freshly ground black pepper. Reheat gently and serve hot.

4 red capsicums (peppers)
4 tomatoes
60 ml (2 fl oz/¼ cup) oil
½ teaspoon dried marjoram
½ teaspoon dried mixed herbs
2 garlic cloves, crushed
1 teaspoon mild curry paste
1 red onion, sliced
1 leek, white part only, sliced
250 g (9 oz) green cabbage, chopped
1 teaspoon sweet chilli sauce

Cannellini bean soup

»PREPARATION 20 MINUTES »COOKING TIME 1 HOUR 15 MINUTES »SERVES 8

1 Put the beans in a bowl, cover with cold water and leave the beans to soak overnight.

2 Score a cross in the base of each tomato. Put in a heatproof bowl and cover with boiling water. Leave for 30 seconds then transfer to cold water and peel the skin away from the cross. Roughly chop the flesh.

3 Drain the beans and rinse under cold water. Heat the oil in a large deep saucepan. Add the onion, reduce the heat and cook gently for 10 minutes, stirring occasionally.

4 Stir in the garlic and cook for 1 minute. Add the cannellini beans, chopped tomato, tomato passata, carrot, celery, stock and bay leaves and stir. Bring to the boil, then reduce the heat to medium–low and simmer, covered, for 45–60 minutes, or until the beans are tender.

5 Just before serving, stir in the lemon juice and season to taste. Stir in some of the parsley and use the rest as a garnish.

500 g (1 lb 2 oz) dried cannellini beans
450 g (1 lb) ripe tomatoes
2 tablespoons olive oil
2 onions, chopped
2 garlic cloves, crushed
3 tablespoons tomato passata (puréed tomatoes)
2 large carrots, diced
2 celery stalks, trimmed and diced
1.7 litres (59 fl oz) vegetable stock
2 bay leaves
2 tablespoons lemon juice
30 g (1 oz) chopped flat-leaf (Italian) parsley

Green papaya salad

»PREPARATION 25 MINUTES »COOKING TIME 5 MINUTES »SERVES 6

1 Grate the papaya, sprinkle with salt and leave for 30 minutes, then rinse well.

2 Cook the beans in a saucepan of boiling water for 3 minutes, or until tender. Drain, plunge into cold water, then drain again.

3 To make the dressing, combine all the ingredients in a small bowl. Set aside.

4 Using a large mortar and pestle, pound the garlic and chilli until crushed. Add the dried shrimp and pound until puréed. Add the papaya and snake beans and lightly pound for 1 minute. Add the tomato and pound briefly to bruise.

5 Combine the coriander sprigs with the papaya mixture and spoon onto serving plates. Drizzle with the dressing. Sprinkle with the peanuts and, if desired, sliced red chilli.

370 g (13 oz) green papaya, peeled and seeded
90 g (3 1/4 oz) snake beans, trimmed and cut into 2 cm (3/4 inch) lengths
2 garlic cloves
2 small red chillies, chopped
5 teaspoons dried shrimp
8 cherry tomatoes, halved
50 g (1 3/4 oz) coriander (cilantro) sprigs
40 g (1 1/2 oz/1/4 cup) chopped roasted peanuts

Dressing

60 ml (2 fl oz/1/4 cup) fish sauce
2 tablespoons tamarind purée
1 tablespoon lime juice
3 tablespoons grated palm sugar (jaggery) or soft brown sugar

Cucumber, feta and mint salad

»PREPARATION 15 MINUTES »COOKING TIME NIL »SERVES 4

1 Crumble the feta into 1 cm (½ inch) pieces and put in a large bowl. Peel and seed the cucumbers and cut into 1 cm (½ inch) cubes. Add to the bowl along with the onion and dill.

2 Grind the mint using a mortar and pestle, or force through a sieve, until powdered. Combine with the oil and juice, then season. Pour over the salad and toss well.

120 g (4 oz) feta cheese
4 Lebanese (short) cucumbers
1 small red onion, thinly sliced
1½ tablespoons finely chopped dill
1 tablespoon dried mint
60 ml (2 fl oz/¼ cup) olive oil
1½ tablespoons lemon juice

66 **Potato noodles with vegetables**

64 **Wild rice, thyme and mixed mushroom pilaf**

72 **Vegetable lasagne**

81 Japanese vegetables with egg

89 Lima bean casserole

Mains

Buddhist vegetarian noodles

»PREPARATION 25 MINUTES »COOKING TIME 15 MINUTES »SERVES 4

15 g (1/2 oz) dried shiitake mushrooms
1 small carrot
150 g (5 1/2 oz) baby corn
225 g (8 oz) tinned bamboo shoots
150 g (5 1/2 oz) snow peas (mangetout)
1/2 small red capsicum (pepper)
1 small green capsicum (pepper)
40 g (1 1/2 oz) Chinese cabbage (wong bok)
400 g (14 oz) fresh flat egg noodles
2–3 tablespoons peanut oil
90 g (3 1/4 oz/1 cup) bean sprouts, trimmed
1 tablespoon thin strips fresh ginger
2 tablespoons vegetarian oyster sauce (see Notes)
1 tablespoon mushroom soy sauce (see Notes)
1 tablespoon light soy sauce
1 tablespoon Chinese rice wine
1 teaspoon sesame oil
ground white pepper, to taste
coriander (cilantro) leaves, to garnish

1 Soak the mushrooms in boiling water for 20 minutes, then drain. Discard the woody stalks and thinly slice the caps.

2 Cut the carrot into thin batons. Quarter the baby corn lengthways. Drain the bamboo shoots and cut them into thin batons. Cut the snow peas into thin batons. Halve the capsicums, remove the seeds and membrane and cut into thin batons. Finely shred the Chinese cabbage.

3 Add the egg noodles to a large saucepan of boiling water and cook for 1 minute, stirring to separate the noodles. Drain, rinse under cold running water and drain again.

4 Heat a wok over high heat, add 1 tablespoon of the oil and swirl to coat the base and side. Stir-fry the carrot and corn for 1–2 minutes, then add the bamboo shoots and stir-fry for a further 1–2 minutes, or until just cooked but still crisp. Remove all of the vegetables from the wok.

5 Reheat the wok (add 2 teaspoons peanut oil if necessary) and add the snow peas and the red and green capsicum. Stir-fry for 1–2 minutes, or until just cooked but still crisp. Add to the carrot and corn mixture.

6 Reheat the wok (add another 2 teaspoons peanut oil if needed), then add the bean sprouts, Chinese cabbage and sliced mushrooms and stir-fry for 30 seconds, until wilted. Add the ginger strips and stir-fry for 1–2 minutes. Remove from the wok and add to the other vegetables.

7 Heat the remaining oil in the wok and quickly stir-fry the noodles for 1–2 minutes, or until they are heated through, taking care not to let them break up. Stir in the vegetarian oyster sauce, mushroom soy sauce, light soy sauce and Chinese rice wine and stir thoroughly. Return all the vegetables to the wok and gently stir for 1–2 minutes, or until well combined with the noodles. Drizzle with the sesame oil, season with white pepper and garnish with the coriander. Serve immediately.

Notes Chillies, garlic, onions and spring onions have been omitted from this recipe because traditional Chinese vegetarians do not eat them.

Vegetarian oyster sauce and mushroom soy sauce are available from Asian food stores.

Spiced carrot and feta gnocchi

»PREPARATION 45 MINUTES »COOKING TIME 40 MINUTES »SERVES 6–8

1 Cut the carrots into large pieces and steam, boil or microwave until tender. Drain and cool slightly, then transfer to a food processor.

2 Process the carrot and feta until smooth and transfer the mixture to a large bowl. Stir in the sifted flour, spices and egg, and mix to form a soft dough.

3 Lightly coat your fingertips with flour and shape teaspoons of the mixture into flat circles.

4 To make the minted cream sauce, melt the butter in a frying pan and cook the garlic and spring onion over medium heat for 3 minutes, or until the garlic is soft and golden. Add the cream and bring to the boil, then reduce the heat and simmer for 3 minutes, until the cream has thickened slightly. Remove from the heat and stir through the mint.

5 Bring a large saucepan of salted water to the boil. Cook the gnocchi, in batches, for about 2 minutes, or until they float to the surface. Use a slotted spoon to transfer to warmed serving plates. Drizzle the sauce over the gnocchi and serve.

Note The gnocchi mixture is not as firm as some other gnocchi recipes. Make sure you work with the dough on a lightly floured surface and keep your fingertips coated in flour when you are shaping the gnocchi.

1 kg (2 lb 4 oz) carrots
200 g (7 oz) feta cheese, crumbled
280 g (10 oz/2¼ cups) plain (all-purpose) flour
¼ teaspoon ground nutmeg
¼ teaspoon garam masala
1 egg, lightly beaten

Minted cream sauce

30 g (1 oz) butter
2 garlic cloves, crushed
2 spring onions (scallions), sliced
250 ml (9 fl oz/1 cup) cream
2 tablespoons shredded mint

Tofu, peanut and noodle stir-fry

»PREPARATION 15 MINUTES »COOKING TIME 5 MINUTES »SERVES 4

1 Cut the capsicum in half, remove the seeds and membrane and chop. Cut the tofu into cubes. Chop the onion, and cut the broccoli into small florets.

2 Combine the tofu with the garlic, ginger and half the kecap manis in a small bowl. Put the peanut butter, 125 ml (4 fl oz/½ cup) water and the remaining kecap manis in another bowl and mix.

3 Heat a wok over high heat, add the oil and swirl to coat. Drain the tofu, reserving the marinade, and cook in two batches until well browned. Remove from the wok.

4 Soak the hokkien noodles in boiling water for 1 minute. Drain and gently separate the noodles. Add the vegetables to the wok (add a little more oil if necessary) and stir-fry until just tender. Add the fried tofu, reserved marinade, noodles and peanut butter mixture to the wok and toss until the tofu and noodles are heated through.

Note Kecap manis is an Indonesian sweet soy sauce. If you are unable to find it, use soy sauce sweetened with a little soft brown sugar.

- 1 red capsicum (pepper)
- 250 g (9 oz) firm tofu
- 1 onion
- 125 g (4½ oz) broccoli
- 2 garlic cloves, crushed
- 1 teaspoon grated fresh ginger
- 80 ml (2½ fl oz/⅓ cup) kecap manis (see Note)
- 90 g (3¼ oz/⅓ cup) peanut butter
- 2 tablespoons peanut or vegetable oil
- 500 g (1 lb 2 oz) hokkien (egg) noodles

Chilli noodles

»PREPARATION 15 MINUTES
»COOKING TIME 10 MINUTES »SERVES 4

1 Chop 200 g (7 oz) thin noodles, then add them to a large saucepan of simmering water and cook until just tender, then drain.

2 Cut 3 red chillies into strips. Heat 60 ml (2 fl oz/¼ cup) vegetable oil and 2 teaspoons chilli oil and in a wok, add the chilli and cook over medium heat for 1 minute. Add 80 g (2¾ oz/½ cup) roasted cashew nuts and toss for 1 minute, until golden.

3 Add 1 thinly sliced red capsicum, 2 sliced celery stalks, 225 g (8 oz) tinned baby corn, 2 tablespoons chopped spring onions (scallions) and 100 g (3½ oz) bean sprouts to the wok and cook for 3 minutes, or until tender.

4 Combine 1 tablespoon soy sauce and 2 tablespoons sweet chilli sauce. Add the sauce and noodles to the wok and toss until the noodles are heated through and the ingredients are combined. Serve.

Egg noodle mix

»PREPARATION 10 MINUTES
»COOKING TIME 10 MINUTES »SERVES 4

1 Cook 375 g (13 oz) thin fresh egg noodles in boiling water until just tender. Drain.

2 Rinse 1 tablespoon dried, salted black beans, then chop them. Heat 1 teaspoon olive oil and 1 teaspoon sesame oil in a wok or frying pan. Stir-fry 1 tablespoon grated fresh ginger and 4 crushed garlic cloves over low heat for 2 minutes. Add the black beans and cook for 2 minutes.

3 Add 125 ml (4 fl oz/½ cup) of vegetable stock, 1 tablespoon black bean sauce, 2 tablespoons hoisin sauce and 1 tablespoon sugar to the wok. Simmer for 5 minutes, or until the mixture is slightly reduced and thickened. Drain 235 g (8½ oz) tinned sliced bamboo shoots and add to the wok with 3 sliced spring onions (scallions) and the noodles. Stir until heated through and all the ingredients are well combined.

Note Dried, salted black beans are available from Asian food stores.

Noodle stir-fry

»PREPARATION 15 MINUTES
»COOKING TIME 10 MINUTES »SERVES 4

1 Combine 2 tablespoons Japanese soy sauce, 2 tablespoons mirin and 2 tablespoons of kecap manis. Cut 6 spring onions (scallions), 500 g (1 lb 2 oz) choy sum and 2 carrots into 5 cm (2 inch) lengths. Cut 150 g (5½ oz) snow peas (mangetout) in half, diagonally.

2 Add 500 g (1 lb 2 oz) fresh udon noodles to a saucepan of boiling water and cook for 1–2 minutes, or until tender and separated. Drain and rinse under hot water.

3 Heat 1 tablespoon oil in a wok over high heat. Stir-fry the spring onion, 3 crushed garlic cloves and 1 tablespoon grated fresh ginger for 2 minutes. Add the carrot, snow peas and 1 tablespoon water, toss well, cover and cook for 1–2 minutes, or until the vegetables are just tender. Add the noodles, choy sum, 100 g (3½ oz) bean sprouts and the sauce. Toss until the choy sum is wilted. Stir in 2 sheets roasted nori, cut into thin strips, just before serving.

Asian mushroom risotto

»PREPARATION 20 MINUTES »COOKING TIME 45 MINUTES »SERVES 4

1 Put the Chinese mushrooms in a bowl, cover with the boiling water and soak for 30 minutes, then drain, reserving the liquid. Remove and discard the stems and thinly slice the caps. Finely chop the onion.

2 Heat the vegetable stock, soy sauce, mirin, reserved mushroom liquid and 250 ml (9 fl oz/1 cup) water in a large saucepan, bring to the boil, then reduce the heat and keep at a low simmer, skimming off any scum that forms on the surface.

3 Trim and slice the Swiss brown, oyster and shiitake mushrooms, discarding any woody ends. Trim the shimeji mushrooms and pull them apart into small clumps. Melt 1 tablespoon of the butter in a large saucepan over medium heat, add all the mushrooms except the Chinese and enoki and cook, stirring, for 3 minutes, or until wilted. Remove from the pan.

4 Heat the oil and remaining butter in the same pan over medium heat, add the onion and cook, stirring, for 4–5 minutes, or until the onion is soft and just starting to brown. Add the garlic and ginger and stir well until fragrant. Add the rice and stir for 1 minute, or until it is well coated in the oil mixture.

5 Gradually add 125 ml (4 fl oz/ ½ cup) of the hot stock to the rice. Stir constantly over medium heat until nearly all the liquid has been absorbed. Add more stock, 125 ml (4 fl oz/½ cup) at a time, stirring constantly for 20–25 minutes, or until all of the stock has been absorbed and the rice is tender.

6 Add all the mushrooms and stir well. Season to taste. Garnish with the chives and shaved parmesan and serve.

10g (¼ oz) dried Chinese mushrooms
625 ml (21½ fl oz/2½ cups) boiling water
1 onion
500 ml (17 fl oz/2 cups) vegetable stock
2 tablespoons soy sauce
80 ml (2½ fl oz/⅓ cup) mirin
150 g (5½ oz) Swiss brown mushrooms
150 g (5½ oz) oyster mushrooms
100 g (3½ oz) fresh shiitake mushrooms
150 g (5½ oz) shimeji mushrooms
40 g (1½ oz) butter
1 tablespoon olive oil
3 garlic cloves, crushed
1 tablespoon finely chopped fresh ginger
440 g (15½ oz/2 cups) arborio rice
100 g (3½ oz) enoki mushrooms, trimmed
2 tablespoons snipped chives
parmesan cheese shavings, to garnish (optional)

Wild rice, thyme and mixed mushroom pilaf

»PREPARATION 20 MINUTES »COOKING TIME 45 MINUTES »SERVES 4

1 Rinse the wild rice and cook in a saucepan of plenty of boiling water for 25 minutes (the rice will only be partially cooked). Drain.

2 When the rice is nearly done, pour the stock into a large saucepan with 375 ml (13 fl oz/1½ cups) of water and bring to the boil. Reduce the heat to a simmer.

3 Meanwhile, finely chop the onion and slice the mushrooms. Melt the butter in a large heavy-based frying pan, add the onion and garlic and cook until the onion is softened but not browned. Add the white rice and stir until the rice is coated with butter, then stir in the mushrooms.

4 Add the wild rice, stock, thyme and bay leaf. Bring to the boil while stirring, then reduce the heat, cover tightly and simmer for 15 minutes, or until the rice is tender and the stock has been absorbed.

5 Leave to stand for 5 minutes. Remove the bay leaf. Season then add the parsley and fluff up the rice with a fork. Sprinkle with pine nuts and serve.

Note Toast the pine nuts in a dry frying pan over medium heat, stirring constantly, until they are golden brown and fragrant. Watch carefully as they will burn easily.

125 g (4½ oz/⅔ cup) wild rice
375 ml (13 fl oz/1½ cups) vegetable stock
1 large onion
300 g (10½ oz) mixed mushrooms (such as button, field, Swiss brown)
60 g (2¼ oz) butter
2 garlic cloves, crushed
265 g (9½ oz/1⅓ cups) long-grain white rice
1½ tablespoons chopped thyme
1 bay leaf
2 tablespoons chopped flat-leaf (Italian) parsley
toasted pine nuts, to serve (see Note)

Tortellini with eggplant

»PREPARATION 10 MINUTES »COOKING TIME 20 MINUTES »SERVES 4

1 red capsicum (pepper)
500 g (1 lb 2 oz) eggplant (aubergine)
500 g (1 lb 2 oz) fresh cheese and spinach tortellini
60 ml (2 fl oz/1/4 cup) oil
2 garlic cloves, crushed
425 g (15 oz) tinned crushed tomatoes
250 ml (9 fl oz/1 cup) vegetable stock
25 g (1 oz) chopped basil

1 Cut the red capsicum in half, remove the seeds and membrane and cut into small squares. Cut the eggplant into small cubes.

2 Cook the tortellini in a large saucepan of rapidly boiling salted water until al dente. Drain and return to the pan.

3 Meanwhile, heat the oil in a large frying pan over medium heat, add the garlic and red capsicum and stir for 1 minute. Add the eggplant to the frying pan and stir gently over medium heat for 5 minutes, or until lightly browned.

4 Add the tomatoes and stock to the pan. Stir and bring to the boil. Reduce the heat to low, cover the pan and cook for 10 minutes, or until the vegetables are tender. Add the basil and pasta and stir until mixed through.

Note Cut the eggplant just before using, as it turns brown when exposed to the air.

Potato noodles with vegetables

»PREPARATION 25 MINUTES
»COOKING TIME 15 MINUTES »SERVES 4

1 Cook 300 g (10½ oz) dried potato starch noodles in a large saucepan of boiling water for about 5 minutes, or until they are translucent. Drain and rinse under cold running water until the noodles are cold (this will also remove any excess starch). Use scissors to roughly chop the noodles into shorter lengths (this will make them easier to eat with chopsticks).

2 Pour hot water over 10 g (¼ oz/⅓ cup) black fungus and soak for 10 minutes.

3 Grate a 4 cm (1½ inch) piece of fresh ginger. Cut 2 carrots into 4 cm (1½ inch) batons. Heat 1 tablespoon of sesame oil and 2 tablespoons of vegetable oil in a large heavy-based frying pan or wok. Add the ginger, 3 finely chopped garlic cloves and 2 finely chopped spring onions (scallions) and cook over medium heat for 3 minutes, stirring regularly. Add the carrot batons and stir-fry for 1 minute.

4 Add the noodles, 2 sliced spring onions, 500 g (1 lb 2 oz) roughly chopped baby bok choy (pak choy), 2 tablespoons sesame oil, 60 ml (2 fl oz/¼ cup) Japanese soy sauce, 2 tablespoons mirin and 1 teaspoon sugar. Toss well to coat the noodles with the sauce. Cover and cook over low heat for 2 minutes. Add the drained fungus, cover and cook for 2 minutes. Scatter over 2 tablespoons sesame and seaweed sprinkle and serve immediately.

Note Potato starch noodles, dried black fungus, Japanese soy sauce, and sesame and seaweed sprinkle are available at Asian food stores.

Fettucine with green olives

»PREPARATION 20 MINUTES »COOKING TIME 20 MINUTES »SERVES 4

1 Cook 500 g (1 lb 2 oz) fettucine or tagliatelle in a large saucepan of rapidly boiling salted water until al dente. Drain and return to the pan.

2 While the pasta is cooking, slice 175 g (6 oz) green olives and cut 1 large eggplant (aubergine) into small cubes.

3 Heat 2 tablespoons olive oil in a heavy-based frying pan and cook 2 crushed garlic cloves, stirring, for 30 seconds. Add the eggplant and cook over medium heat, stirring frequently, for 6 minutes, or until tender. Add the olives and 125 ml (4 fl oz/½ cup) lemon juice and season to taste. Add the sauce to the pasta and toss to combine. Sprinkle with 2 tablespoons of chopped flat-leaf (Italian) parsley and 50 g (1¾ oz/½ cup) freshly grated parmesan cheese.

Sweet potato and spinach stir-fry

»PREPARATION 15 MINUTES »COOKING TIME 20 MINUTES »SERVES 4

1 Cut the sweet potato into small cubes. Cook in a large saucepan of boiling water for 15 minutes, or until tender. Drain well. Slice the water chestnuts.

2 Heat a wok over high heat, add the oil and swirl to coat the base and side. Stir-fry the garlic and sambal oelek for 1 minute, or until fragrant. Add the sweet potato and water chestnuts and stir-fry over medium–high heat for 2 minutes. Reduce the heat to medium, add the palm sugar and cook for 2 minutes, or until the sugar has melted. Add the spinach, soy sauce and stock and toss until the spinach has just wilted. Serve with steamed rice.

Note Sambal oelek is a Southeast Asian chilli paste.

- 500 g (1 lb 2 oz) orange sweet potato
- 225 g (8 oz) tinned water chestnuts
- 1 tablespoon oil
- 2 garlic cloves, crushed
- 2 teaspoons sambal oelek (see Note)
- 2 teaspoons grated palm sugar (jaggery) or soft brown sugar
- 400 g (14 oz) English spinach, stems removed
- 2 tablespoons soy sauce
- 2 tablespoons vegetable stock

Indonesian coconut and spice rice

»PREPARATION 15 MINUTES »COOKING TIME 20 MINUTES »SERVES 4

1 Heat the oil in a wok. Add the peanuts and cook, stirring often, until they turn golden brown. Add the coconut and stir until it darkens slightly and becomes fragrant.

2 Pour the coconut milk and 500 ml (17 fl oz/2 cups) water into the wok. Add the lemon grass, curry leaves and spring onion, then bring to the boil. Reduce the heat and simmer for 2 minutes. Add the cardamom, cumin and turmeric, and bring to the boil again. Lift out the lemon grass stem, then add the rice and cook until steam holes appear at the surface of the rice.

3 Cover the wok with a tight-fitting lid, reduce the heat to very low and cook for 10 minutes. Lift the lid and check if the rice is cooked. Continue cooking (with the lid on) if required.

Notes Basmati or jasmine rice can be used instead of long-grain rice, if you prefer.

Avoid lifting the lid while the rice is cooking, as all the steam will escape, resulting in thick, starchy rice.

1 tablespoon oil

80 g (2¾ oz/½ cup) peanuts, roughly chopped

1 tablespoon shredded coconut

250 ml (9 fl oz/1 cup) coconut milk

10 cm (4 inch) lemon grass stem, white part only, lightly crushed with the side of a knife

8 curry leaves

2 spring onions (scallions), cut into 2.5 mm (⅛ inch) slices.

½ teaspoon ground cardamom

1 teaspoon ground cumin

½ teaspoon ground turmeric

500 g (1 lb 2 oz/2½ cups) long-grain rice

Pumpkin gnocchi with sage butter

»PREPARATION 45 MINUTES »COOKING TIME 1 HOUR 30 MINUTES »SERVES 4

500 g (1 lb 2 oz) pumpkin (winter squash), unpeeled

185 g (6½ oz/1½ cups) plain (all-purpose) flour

50 g (1¾ oz/½ cup) freshly grated parmesan cheese

1 egg, beaten

100 g (3½ oz) butter

2 tablespoons chopped sage

sage leaves, to garnish

1 Preheat the oven to 160°C (315°F/Gas 2–3). Brush a baking tray with some oil or melted butter. Cut the pumpkin into large pieces, leaving the skin on, and put on the tray. Bake the pumpkin for 1¼ hours, or until very tender. Cool slightly. Scrape the flesh from the skin, avoiding any tough or crisp parts. Transfer to a large bowl. Sift the flour into the bowl, add half the parmesan, the egg and a little black pepper. Mix thoroughly, then turn onto a lightly floured surface and knead for 2 minutes, until smooth.

2 Divide the dough in half. Using floured hands, roll each half into a sausage shape 40 cm (16 inches) long. Cut into 16 equal pieces, then form each piece into an oval shape and press firmly with the floured prongs of a fork to make a clear indentation.

3 Lower batches of the gnocchi into a large saucepan of boiling salted water. Cook for about 2 minutes, or until the gnocchi rise to the surface. Drain with a slotted spoon and keep them warm.

4 To make the sage butter, melt the butter in a small frying pan, remove from the heat and stir in the sage.

5 Divide the gnocchi among four serving bowls and drizzle with the sage butter. Sprinkle with the rest of the parmesan and garnish with the sage leaves.

Fettucine with creamy mushroom and bean sauce

»PREPARATION 20 MINUTES »COOKING TIME 20 MINUTES »SERVES 4

1 Cook the fettucine in a large saucepan of rapidly boiling salted water until al dente. Drain, return to the pan and keep warm.

2 Cut the sun-dried tomatoes and beans into thin strips. Thinly slice the mushrooms.

3 Heat the oil in a large heavy-based frying pan. Cook the onion and garlic over medium heat for 3 minutes, or until softened. Add the sliced mushrooms and cook, stirring, for 1 minute. Add the wine, cream and stock. Bring to the boil, then reduce the heat and simmer for 10 minutes.

4 Lightly beat the egg in a small bowl. Stirring constantly, add a little of the cooking liquid to the egg. Pour the mixture slowly into the frying pan, stirring constantly for 30 seconds. Keep the heat low because the mixture will curdle if it boils.

5 Add the beans, basil, pine nuts and sun-dried tomato and stir until heated through. Season to taste.

6 Serve the sauce over the pasta, garnished with parmesan shavings and sprigs of fresh herbs, if desired.

Note Toast the pine nuts in a dry frying pan over medium heat, stirring constantly, until they are golden brown and fragrant. Watch carefully as they will burn easily.

280 g (10 oz) fettucine
35 g (1 1/4 oz/1/4 cup) sun-dried tomatoes
250 g (9 oz) green beans, trimmed
250 g (9 oz) mushrooms
2 tablespoons oil
1 onion, chopped
2 garlic cloves, crushed
125 ml (4 fl oz/1/2 cup) white wine
310 ml (10 3/4 oz/1 1/4 cups) cream
125 ml (4 fl oz/1/2 cup) vegetable stock
1 egg
3 tablespoons chopped basil
100 g (3 1/2 oz/2/3 cup) pine nuts, toasted (See Note)
50 g (1 3/4 oz) shaved parmesan cheese
herb sprigs, to serve (optional)

Vegetable lasagne

»PREPARATION 40 MINUTES »COOKING TIME 1 HOUR 15 MINUTES »SERVES 6

3 large red capsicums (peppers)
1 large onion
500 g (1 lb 2 oz) English spinach
500 g (1 lb 2 oz) mushrooms
90 g (3¼ oz) sun-dried tomatoes
2 large eggplants (aubergines)
2 tablespoons oil
3 garlic cloves, crushed
1 teaspoon dried mixed herbs
1 teaspoon dried oregano
440 g (15½ oz) tinned crushed tomatoes
440 g (15½ oz) tinned red kidney beans, drained
1 tablespoon sweet chilli sauce
250 g (9 oz) packet instant lasagne
30 g (1 oz) basil leaves
25 g (1 oz/¼ cup) grated parmesan cheese
30 g (1 oz/¼ cup) grated cheddar cheese

Cheese sauce

60 g (2¼ oz) butter
30 g (1 oz/¼ cup) plain (all-purpose) flour
500 ml (17 fl oz/2 cups) milk
600 g (1 lb 5 oz) ricotta cheese

1 Preheat the oven to 180°C (350°F/Gas 4). Brush a 28 x 35 cm (11¼ x 14 inch) ovenproof dish with oil.

2 Cut the capsicum in half, remove the seeds and membrane and cut into large flattish pieces. Cook, skin side up, under a hot grill (broiler) for 8 minutes, or until the skin is black and blistered. Cover with a damp tea towel (dish towel) and leave to cool, then peel away the skin and cut the flesh into long thin strips. Set aside. Chop the onion and the English spinach. Slice the mushrooms and the sun-dried tomatoes.

3 Slice the eggplant into 1 cm (½ inch) rounds and put in a large saucepan of boiling water. Cook for 1 minute, or until just tender. Drain, then pat dry with paper towel and set aside.

4 Heat the oil in a large heavy-based frying pan over medium heat. Cook the onion, garlic and herbs for 5 minutes, or until the onion is soft. Add the sliced mushrooms and cook for 1 minute.

5 Add the tomatoes, red kidney beans and chilli sauce, and season to taste. Bring to the boil, reduce the heat and simmer for 15 minutes, or until the sauce thickens. Remove from the heat and set aside.

6 To make the cheese sauce, heat the butter in a saucepan and stir in the flour over medium heat for 1 minute, or until smooth. Remove from the heat and gradually stir in the milk. Return to the heat and stir constantly until the sauce boils and begins to thicken. Reduce the heat and simmer for 1 minute. Add the ricotta and stir until smooth.

7 Dip the instand lasagne sheets, if necessary, in hot water to soften slightly and arrange four sheets on the base of the prepared dish. Build up layers on top of the pasta, using half of the eggplant, the spinach, the basil, the grilled capsicum strips, the mushroom sauce and then the sun-dried tomatoes. Top with a layer of lasagne and press gently. Repeat the layers, finishing with a layer of lasagne. Spoon the cheese sauce over the lasagne. Sprinkle with the combined grated parmesan and cheddar cheeses and bake for 45 minutes, or until the pasta is soft.

Spinach and ricotta gnocchi

»PREPARATION 45 MINUTES »COOKING TIME 30 MINUTES »SERVES 4–6

1 Remove the crust from the bread and place in a shallow dish. Pour the milk over the bread and soak for 10 minutes, then squeeze out all the excess liquid.

2 Squeeze the excess liquid from the spinach. Combine the spinach in a bowl with the bread, ricotta, eggs and parmesan, then season. Use a fork to mix thoroughly. Cover and refrigerate for 1 hour.

3 Lightly dust your hands in the flour. Roll heaped teaspoonsful of the mixture into dumplings. Lower batches of the gnocchi into a large saucepan of boiling salted water. Cook for 2 minutes, or until the gnocchi rise to the surface. Transfer to serving plates and drizzle with foaming butter, if you wish, and serve with the parmesan shavings.

4 slices white bread
125 ml (4 fl oz/½ cup) milk
500 g (1 lb 2 oz) frozen spinach, thawed
250 g (9 oz/1 cup) ricotta cheese
2 eggs
50 g (1¾ oz/½ cup) freshly grated parmesan cheese
30 g (1 oz/¼ cup) plain (all-purpose) flour
parmesan cheese shavings, to serve

Brown rice and puy lentils

»PREPARATION 15 MINUTES »COOKING TIME 40 MINUTES »SERVES 6–8

1 Score a cross in the base of each tomato. Put in a heatproof bowl and cover with boiling water. Leave for 30 seconds, then transfer to cold water, drain and peel away the skin. Cut the tomatoes in half, scoop out all the seeds and dice the flesh. Dice the onion, carrot and celery.

2 Bring a large saucepan of water to the boil. Add 1 teaspoon salt and the rice, and cook for 20 minutes, or until tender. Drain and refresh under cold water.

3 Heat 2 tablespoons of the oil in a saucepan and add the onion, garlic, carrot and celery. Cook over low heat for 5 minutes, or until softened, then add the puy lentils and 375 ml (13 fl oz/1½ cups) water. Bring to the boil and simmer for 15 minutes, or until tender. Drain well, but do not rinse. Transfer to a large bowl.

4 Add the rice, tomato, coriander and mint to the lentils. Whisk the remaining oil with the vinegar and lemon juice and season well. Pour over the salad, add the pine nuts and spinach, and toss to combine.

Note Toast the pine nuts in a dry frying pan over medium heat, stirring constantly, until they are golden brown and fragrant.

- 2 tomatoes
- 1 red onion
- 1 carrot
- 2 celery stalks
- 200 g (7 oz/1 cup) long-grain brown rice
- 100 ml (3½ fl oz) extra virgin olive oil
- 2 garlic cloves, crushed
- 200 g (7 oz/1 cup) puy lentils
- 3 tablespoons chopped coriander (cilantro)
- 3 tablespoons chopped mint
- 2 tablespoons balsamic vinegar
- 1 tablespoon lemon juice
- 2 tablespoons pine nuts, toasted (see Note)
- 100 g (3½ oz/2 cups) baby English spinach leaves

Indian spiced rice

»PREPARATION 20 MINUTES »COOKING TIME 15 MINUTES »SERVES 6

1 Wash the rice in a sieve under cold water until the water from the rice runs clear. Drain the rice and put in a saucepan. Cover with water and soak for 30 minutes. Drain.

2 Dry-fry the cumin seeds in a small frying pan over low heat until they are aromatic.

3 Heat the ghee or oil in a karhai (Indian wok) or heavy-based frying pan and fry the almonds and raisins until browned. Remove from the pan. Fry the onion in the same ghee until it is dark golden brown, then remove from the pan.

4 Add the rice, roasted cumin, cinnamon, cardamom, sugar, ginger juice, saffron and some salt to the frying pan and fry for 2 minutes, or until aromatic.

5 Add the bay leaves and coconut milk to the pan, then add enough water to come about 5 cm (2 inches) above the rice. Bring to the boil, cover and cook over medium heat for 8 minutes, or until most of the water has evaporated.

6 Add the peas to the pan and stir well. Reduce the heat to very low and cook until the rice is cooked through. Stir in the fried almonds, raisins and onion, reserving some for garnishing. Drizzle with a few drops of rosewater if you would like a more perfumed dish. Garnish with the reserved almonds, raisins and onion, then serve.

Note Indian bay leaves (cassia leaves) are available from Asian speciality food stores.

500 g (1 lb 2 oz/2½ cups) basmati rice
1 teaspoon cumin seeds
60 ml (2 fl oz/¼ cup) ghee or oil
2 tablespoons chopped almonds
2 tablespoons raisins or sultanas (golden raisins)
2 onions, thinly sliced
2 cinnamon sticks
5 cardamom pods
1 teaspoon sugar
1 tablespoon ginger juice
15 saffron threads, soaked in 1 tablespoon warm milk
2 Indian bay leaves (cassia leaves) (see Note)
250 ml (9 fl oz/1 cup) coconut milk
2 tablespoons fresh or frozen peas
rosewater (optional)

Fettucine with zucchini and basil

»PREPARATION 15 MINUTES »COOKING TIME 15 MINUTES »SERVES 6

1 To crisp-fry the basil leaves, heat the oil in a small frying pan, add two leaves at a time and cook for 1 minute, or until crisp. Remove with a slotted spoon and drain on paper towel. Repeat with the remaining basil leaves.

2 Cook the fettucine in a large saucepan of rapidly boiling salted water until al dente. Drain and return to the pan.

3 While the pasta is cooking, grate the zucchini. Heat the butter in a deep heavy-based saucepan over low heat until foaming. Add the garlic and cook for 1 minute. Add the zucchini and cook, stirring occasionally, for 1–2 minutes, or until softened. Add to the hot pasta. Add the parmesan and toss well. Serve the pasta garnished with the crisp basil leaves.

Note The basil leaves can be fried up to 2 hours in advance. Store in an airtight container after cooling.

250 ml (9 fl oz/1 cup) olive oil
handful basil leaves
500 g (1 lb 2 oz) fettucine or tagliatelle
500 g (1 lb 2 oz) zucchini (courgettes)
60 g (2¼ oz) butter
2 garlic cloves, crushed
75 g (2¾ oz/¾ cup) freshly grated parmesan cheese

Mushroom nut roast with tomato sauce

»PREPARATION 30 MINUTES
»COOKING TIME 1 HOUR »SERVES 6

1 Lightly grease a 14 x 21 cm (5½ x 8¼ inch) loaf (bar) tin and line the base with baking paper.

2 Dice 1 large onion. Finely chop 300 g (10½ oz) cap mushrooms. Heat 2 tablespoons olive oil in a frying pan and add the onion, mushrooms and 2 crushed garlic cloves. Fry until soft, then cool.

3 Process 200 g (7 oz) cashew nuts and 200 g (7 oz) brazil nuts in a food processor until finely chopped, but do not overprocess. Preheat the oven to 180°C (350°F/Gas 4).

4 Combine the mushroom mixture, chopped nuts, 80 g (2¾ oz/1 cup) fresh wholemeal (whole-wheat) breadcrumbs, 125 g (4½ oz/1 cup) grated cheddar cheese, 25 g (¾ oz/ ¼ cup) freshly grated parmesan cheese, 2 tablespoons snipped chives and 1 lightly beaten egg in a bowl. Mix well and season to taste. Press into the prepared loaf tin and bake for 45 minutes, or until firm. Leave for 5 minutes, then turn out and garnish with chives. Cut into slices to serve.

5 To make the tomato sauce, heat 1½ tablespoons olive oil in a saucepan. Cook 1 finely chopped onion and 1 crushed garlic clove, stirring frequently, for 5 minutes, or until soft but not brown. Stir in 400 g (14 oz) tinned chopped tomatoes, 1 tablespoon tomato paste (concentrated purée), 1 teaspoon caster (superfine) sugar and 80 ml (2½ fl oz/⅓ cup) water. Simmer gently for 3–5 minutes, or until slightly thickened. Season to taste. Serve the tomato sauce with the sliced nut roast.

Add the onion and crushed garlic and fry until soft ...

Indonesian pumpkin curry

»PREPARATION 20 MINUTES »COOKING TIME 25 MINUTES »SERVES 4

1 Combine 3 candlenuts, 2 garlic cloves, 2–3 teaspoons sambal oelek, 1 tablespoon peanuts, 2 red Asian shallots, 1 teaspoon grated fresh galangal and ¼ teaspoon ground turmeric and in a food processor or blender. Process to a smooth paste.

2 Heat a wok over high heat, add 2 tablespoons oil and swirl to coat the base and side. Fry the curry paste, stirring, over low heat for 3–5 minutes, or until fragrant. Add 1 finely chopped onion and cook for 5 minutes.

3 Add 600 g (1 lb 5 oz) cubed butternut pumpkin (squash) and 125 ml (4 fl oz/½ cup) vegetable stock to the wok. Cover and cook for 10 minutes, until the pumpkin is almost cooked through. Pour in more stock, if required. Add 350 g (12 oz) roughly chopped English spinach, 400 ml (14 fl oz) coconut cream and ¼ teaspoon sugar, and season with salt. Bring to the boil, stirring constantly, then reduce the heat and simmer for 3–5 minutes, or until the spinach is cooked and the sauce has thickened slightly

Note Sambal oelek is a Southeast Asian chilli paste.

Pea, egg and ricotta

»PREPARATION 15 MINUTES »COOKING TIME 30 MINUTES »SERVES 4

1 Peel the eggs and coat them with the turmeric. Melt the ghee in a large saucepan and cook the eggs over moderate heat for 2 minutes until they are light brown, stirring constantly. Set aside.

2 Add the bay leaf, onion and garlic to the pan. Cook over moderately high heat, stirring frequently, until the mixture is well-reduced and pale gold. Reduce the heat if the mixture is browning too quickly. Add the ground coriander, garam masala and chilli powder and cook until fragrant.

3 Add the tomatoes, tomato paste and 125 ml (4 fl oz/½ cup) water to the pan. Cover and simmer for 5 minutes. Return the eggs to the pan with the ricotta, yoghurt, peas and ¼ teaspoon salt and cook for 5 minutes. Remove the bay leaf, sprinkle with the coriander and serve immediately.

Note Baked ricotta is available from delicatessens and some large supermarkets. To prepare your own, preheat the oven to 160°C (315°F/Gas 2–3). Slice the required amount of fresh ricotta (not blended ricotta) into 3 cm (1¼ inch) thick slices and place on a lightly greased baking tray. Bake for 25 minutes.

- 4 hard-boiled eggs
- ½ teaspoon ground turmeric
- 45 ml (1½ fl oz) ghee or oil
- 1 bay leaf
- 2 small onions, finely chopped
- 1 teaspoon finely chopped garlic
- 1½ teaspoons ground coriander
- 1½ teaspoons garam masala
- ½ teaspoon chilli powder (optional)
- 125 g (4½ oz/½ cup) tinned peeled, chopped tomatoes
- 1 tablespoon tomato paste (concentrated purée)
- 25 g (4½ oz) baked ricotta cheese, cut into 1 cm (½ inch cubes) (see Note)
- 1 tablespoon plain yoghurt
- 80 g (2¾ oz/½ cup) frozen peas
- 2 tablespoons finely chopped coriander (cilantro) leaves

Japanese vegetables with egg

»PREPARATION 20 MINUTES »COOKING TIME 35 MINUTES »SERVES 4

100 g (3½ oz) green beans
2 slender eggplants (aubergines)
5 spring onions (scallions)
1 onion
440 g (15½ oz/2 cups) Japanese short-grain rice
10 g (¼ oz) dried shiitake mushrooms
420 ml (14½ fl oz/1⅔ cups) boiling water
2 tablespoons oil
100 ml (3½ fl oz) Japanese soy sauce (see Note)
100 ml (3½ fl oz) mirin
55 g (2 oz/¼ cup) sugar
4 eggs, lightly beaten

1 Trim the green beans and cut them into 4 cm (1½ inch) lengths. Slice the eggplants diagonally and cut the spring onions into 2 cm (¾ inch) lengths. Slice the onion.

2 Wash the rice and put it in a saucepan with 625 ml (21½ fl oz/ 2½ cups) water. Bring to the boil then reduce the heat and simmer, covered, for 15 minutes. Remove from the heat, cover and set aside for 10 minutes.

3 Meanwhile, soak the mushrooms in the boiling water for 15 minutes. Drain and reserve the soaking liquid. Remove the stems and cut the caps in half.

4 Heat the oil in a deep frying pan. Cook the onion over medium heat for 4 minutes, or until soft but not browned. Add the eggplant slices and cook for 3–4 minutes, or until softened. Add the mushrooms, beans and spring onion. Cook for 2–3 minutes, until almost cooked. Combine the soy sauce, mushroom soaking liquid, mirin and sugar, and stir through the vegetables. Simmer for 4 minutes.

5 Pour the egg over the vegetables, cover and simmer for 1 minute, or until partly cooked. Serve the rice in bowls, spoon on the vegetable mixture and pour on the cooking sauce from the pan.

Note Japanese soy sauce (Shoyu) is available from Asian speciality food stores.

Individual vegetable pot pies

»PREPARATION 40 MINUTES »COOKING TIME 45 MINUTES »SERVES 6

1 potato
150 g (5½ oz) pumpkin (winter squash)
1 large carrot
1 onion
1 red capsicum (pepper)
150 g (5½ oz) small broccoli florets
1 tablespoon oil
50 g (1¾ oz) butter
2 tablespoons plain (all-purpose) flour
375 ml (13 fl oz/1½ cups) milk
125 g (4½ oz/1 cup) grated cheddar cheese
2 egg yolks
cayenne pepper, to taste
2 sheets ready-rolled puff pastry
1 egg, lightly beaten
1 teaspoon poppy seeds

1 Preheat the oven to 210°C (415°F/Gas 6–7). Brush six 250 ml (9 fl oz/1 cup) capacity ramekins with oil.

2 Cut the potato into small cubes. Cut the pumpkin and carrot into 1 cm (½ inch) cubes. Finely chop the onion. Halve the red capsicum, remove the seeds and membrane and cut into 1 cm (½ inch) squares.

3 Steam or microwave the potato, pumpkin, carrot and broccoli until just tender. Drain well and place in a large bowl. Heat the oil in a frying pan over medium heat and cook the onion and capsicum for 2 minutes, until soft. Add to the bowl.

4 Heat the butter in a saucepan and add the flour. Stir over low heat for 2 minutes, or until lightly golden. Add the milk gradually, stirring until smooth. Stir over medium heat for 3 minutes, or until the mixture boils and thickens. Boil for another minute, then remove from the heat and cool slightly. Stir the cheese and egg yolks into the sauce. Season to taste with cayenne pepper and salt.

5 Add the sauce to the vegetables and stir to combine, then divide the mixture among the ramekins. Cut six circles from the pastry to fit the top of the ramekins. Press the edges to seal, and brush with beaten egg. Sprinkle with poppy seeds. Bake for 30 minutes, or until golden brown.

Note These pies are best eaten on the day they are made.

Sweet vegetable curry

»PREPARATION 20 MINUTES »COOKING TIME 40 MINUTES »SERVES 4

1 Cut the carrots, parsnip and potato into 2 cm (¾ inch) pieces. Cut the capsicum in half, remove the seeds and membrane and cut into 2 cm (¾ inch) squares. Chop the onions and cut the cauliflower into small florets.

2 Heat the oil in a large heavy-based saucepan and cook the onion over medium heat for 4 minutes, or until just soft. Add the cardamom, cumin seeds, coriander, turmeric, mustard seeds, chilli powder, cloves and ginger and cook, stirring, for 1 minute, or until aromatic.

3 Add the carrot, parsnip, potato, vegetable stock, apricot nectar and chutney to the pan. Cook, covered, over medium heat for 25 minutes, stirring occasionally.

4 Add the capsicum, mushrooms and cauliflower and simmer for 10 minutes, or until the vegetables are tender. Stir in the ground almonds and serve with rice.

Note Any vegetables can be used in this curry. For example, broccoli, zucchini (courgette), red capsicum (pepper) or orange sweet potato would be suitable.

2 carrots
1 parsnip
1 potato
1 green capsicum (pepper)
2 onions
300 g (10½ oz) cauliflower
2 tablespoons oil
1 teaspoon ground cardamom
1½ teaspoons cumin seeds
1 teaspoon ground coriander
1 teaspoon ground turmeric
1 teaspoon brown mustard seeds
½ teaspoon chilli powder
¼ teaspoon ground cloves
2 teaspoons grated fresh ginger
330 ml (11¼ fl oz/1⅓ cups) vegetable stock
185 ml (6 fl oz/¾ cup) apricot nectar
2 tablespoons fruit chutney
200 g (7 oz) small button mushrooms
25 g (¾ oz/¼ cup) ground almonds

Tempeh stir-fry

»PREPARATION 15 MINUTES »COOKING TIME 15 MINUTES »SERVES 4

1 Thinly slice the chilli. Slice the spring onions, diagonally. Cut the tempeh into 2 cm (¾ inch) cubes. Chop the Chinese broccoli.

2 Heat a wok over high heat, add the oils and swirl to coat the base and side. Add the garlic, ginger, chilli and spring onion and cook for 1–2 minutes, until the onion is soft. Add the tempeh and cook for 5 minutes, or until golden. Remove from the wok.

3 Add half the Chinese broccoli and bok choy and 1 tablespoon water to the wok and cook, covered, for 3–4 minutes, or until the greens have wilted. Remove from the wok and repeat with the remaining greens and a little more water. Return the greens and tempeh to the wok, add the vegetarian oyster sauce and vinegar and warm through. Top with the coriander and nuts, and serve with rice.

Notes Vegetarian oyster sauce is available from Asian food stores.

Toast the cashew nuts in a dry frying pan over medium heat, stirring constantly, until they are golden brown and fragrant. Watch carefully as they will burn easily.

1 red chilli
4 spring onions (scallions)
300 g (10½ oz) tempeh
800 g (1 lb 12 oz) Chinese broccoli (gai larn)
1 teaspoon sesame oil
1 tablespoon peanut oil
2 garlic cloves, crushed
1 tablespoon grated fresh ginger
500 g (1 lb 2 oz) baby bok choy (pak choy) leaves
125 ml (4 fl oz/½ cup) vegetarian oyster sauce (see Notes)
2 tablespoons rice vinegar
2 tablespoons coriander (cilantro) leaves
40 g (1½ oz/¼ cup) toasted cashew nuts (see Notes)

Almond and broccoli stir-fry

»PREPARATION 10 MINUTES
»COOKING TIME 5 MINUTES »SERVES 4

1 Lightly crush 1 teaspoon coriander seeds using a mortar and pestle or a rolling pin. Cut 500 g (1 lb) broccoli into small florets.

2 Heat 60 ml (2 fl oz/¼ cup) olive oil in a wok or a large heavy-based frying pan and swirl to coat. Add coriander seeds and 2 tablespoons slivered almonds, and stir quickly over medium heat for 1 minute, or until the almonds are golden.

3 Add the broccoli, 1 garlic clove, crushed and 1 teaspoon finely shredded fresh ginger to the pan. Stir-fry over high heat for about 2 minutes, then remove from heat. Combine 2 tablespoons red wine vinegar, 1 tablespoon soy sauce and 2 teaspoons sesame oil and add to the pan. Toss until the broccoli is well coated. Serve at once, sprinkled with toasted sesame seeds.

Baby squash with rice stuffing

»PREPARATION 20 MINUTES
»COOKING TIME 15 MINUTES » MAKES 24

1 Steam 24 baby (pattypan) yellow squash for 5 minutes, or until just tender. Cut a thin slice off the base of each squash, then slice a thin piece off the top for a lid. Using a melon baller, scoop out and discard the flesh, leaving a thin shell.

2 Heat 1 tablespoon oil in a wok and stir-fry 2 teaspoons red curry paste, 1 finely chopped spring onion (scallion) and 1 finely chopped red capsicum (pepper) for 2–3 minutes. Add 185 g (6½ oz/1 cup) cooked jasmine rice and stir-fry for another 2–3 minutes. Add 1 tablespoon of finely chopped coriander (cilantro) leaves and 2 finely shredded makrut (kaffir lime) leaves. Toss to combine.

3 Spoon 1 teaspoon of rice into each of the yellow squash. Garnish with coriander (cilantro) leaves and arrange the lids on top. Arrange on a platter and serve.

Note You will need to cook 65 g (2¼ oz/⅓ cup) of jasmine rice.

Brown rice and tomato tart

»PREPARATION 25 MINUTES »COOKING TIME 2 HOURS 20 MINUTES »SERVES 6

1 Cook 200 g (7 oz/1 cup) brown rice in a saucepan of boiling water for 35 minutes. Drain and set aside. Preheat the oven to 200°C (400°F/Gas 6). Put the rice, 60 g (2¼ oz/½ cup) grated cheddar cheese and 1 lightly beaten egg in a bowl. Mix until well combined. Spread the mixture over the base and side of a greased 25 cm (10 inch) flan tin or quiche dish. Bake for 15 minutes.

2 Halve 6 roma (plum) tomatoes and place on a non-stick baking tray with 6 unpeeled garlic cloves. Brush 1 tablespoon olive oil over the garlic and tomato halves and sprinkle with pepper. Bake for 30 minutes. Cool slightly, then peel the garlic. Reduce the oven to 180°C (350°F/Gas 4).

3 Arrange tomato halves, garlic and 8 lemon thyme sprigs over the rice crust. Crumble 50 g (1¾ oz) goat's cheese on top. Whisk 3 eggs and 60 ml (2 fl oz/¼ cup) milk. Pour over tart. Bake for 1 hour, until set.

Borlotti bean moussaka

»PREPARATION 45 MINUTES »COOKING TIME 2 HOURS 30 MINUTES »SERVES 6

1 Soak the borlotti beans in cold water overnight. Rinse and drain well. Put the borlotti beans in a large heavy-based saucepan, cover with water and bring to the boil. Reduce the heat and simmer for 1½ hours, or until tender. Drain the beans.

2 Meanwhile, slice the eggplant, sprinkle with salt and set aside for 30 minutes. Rinse and pat dry. Brush the eggplant slices with a little of the oil and cook under a hot grill (broiler) for 3 minutes each side, or until golden. Drain on paper towel. Chop the onion and slice the mushrooms.

3 Preheat the oven to 200°C (400°F/Gas 6). Heat the remaining oil in a large heavy-based saucepan. Add the garlic and onion and cook over medium heat for 3 minutes, or until the onion is golden. Add the mushrooms and cook for 3 minutes, or until browned. Stir in the tomato, wine, tomato paste and oregano. Bring to the boil, then reduce the heat and simmer for 40 minutes, or until the sauce has thickened.

4 Spoon the borlotti beans into a large ovenproof dish. Top with the tomato sauce and eggplant slices.

5 To make the topping, whisk together the yoghurt, eggs, milk and paprika. Pour the topping over the eggplant. Set aside for 10 minutes. Combine the parmesan cheese and breadcrumbs and sprinkle over the moussaka. Bake for 45–60 minutes, or until the moussaka is heated through and the top is golden.

250 g (9 oz/1¼ cups) dried borlotti (cranberry) beans
2 large eggplants (aubergines)
80 ml (2½ fl oz/⅓ cup) olive oil
1 onion
125 g (4½ oz) button mushrooms
1 garlic clove, crushed
2 x 440 g (15½ oz) tins peeled tomatoes, chopped
250 ml (9 fl oz/1 cup) red wine
1 tablespoon tomato paste (concentrated purée)
1 tablespoon chopped oregano

Topping

250 g (9 oz/1 cup) plain yoghurt
4 eggs, lightly beaten
500 ml (17 fl oz/2 cups) milk
¼ teaspoon paprika
50 g (1¾ oz/½ cup) freshly grated parmesan cheese
40 g (1½ oz/½ cup) fresh breadcrumbs

Spicy chickpea and vegetable casserole

»PREPARATION 25 MINUTES »COOKING TIME 1 HOUR 30 MINUTES »SERVES 4

1 Put the chickpeas in a large bowl. Cover with cold water and soak overnight. Drain.

2 Chop the onion, cut the pumpkin into large cubes and trim the beans. Cut the button squash into quarters.

3 Heat oil in a large saucepan and stir-fry the onion and garlic for 2 minutes, or until just tender. Add the cumin, chilli and allspice and stir-fry for 1 minute. Add chickpeas, tomatoes and stock to the pan, then bring to the boil. Reduce the heat, cover and simmer for about 1 hour, stirring occasionally.

4 Add the pumpkin, beans, squash, tomato paste and oregano. Stir, then simmer, covered, for 15 minutes. Simmer, uncovered, for another 10 minutes to reduce and slightly thicken the sauce.

Note A quick way to soak chickpeas is to place them in a large saucepan and cover with cold water. Bring to the boil, then remove from the heat and soak for 2 hours. If you are in a hurry, substitute tinned chickpeas. Drain and rinse before use.

- 335 g (11¾ oz/1½ cups) dried chickpeas (see Note)
- 1 large onion
- 300 g (10½ oz) pumpkin (winter squash)
- 150 g (5½ oz) green beans
- 200 g (7 oz) button squash
- 2 tablespoons oil
- 1 garlic clove, crushed
- 3 teaspoons ground cumin
- ½ teaspoon chilli powder
- ½ teaspoon ground allspice
- 425 g (15 oz) tinned peeled tomatoes, crushed
- 375 ml (13 fl oz/1½ cups) vegetable stock
- 2 tablespoons tomato paste (concentrated purée)
- 1 teaspoon dried oregano

Lima bean casserole

»PREPARATION 20 MINUTES »COOKING TIME 2 HOURS »SERVES 6–8

1 Cover the lima beans with cold water and leave to soak overnight. Drain well.

2 Bring a large saucepan of water to the boil, add lima the beans and return to the boil, then reduce the heat to medium and cook, partially covered, for 45–60 minutes, or until the beans are tender but not mushy. Drain. Preheat the oven to 180°C (350°F/Gas 4).

3 Slice the onion and chop the carrot and celery. Heat the oil in a 2.5 litre (88 fl oz/10 cup) flameproof casserole dish over medium heat. Add the onion, garlic, carrot and celery, and cook for 5 minutes, or until the onion is translucent. Add the tomatoes, tomato paste and 125 ml (4 fl oz/½ cup) water. Bring to the boil, then reduce the heat and simmer for 3 minutes.

4 Add the lima beans and dill to the dish, then season to taste. Bring back to the boil, cover and bake for 50 minutes, or until the sauce is thick and the lima beans are soft. Serve hot or at room temperature, drizzled with the oil.

185 g (6½ oz/1 cup) dried lima beans
1 large onion
1 small carrot
1 small celery stalk
60 ml (2 fl oz/¼ cup) olive oil
1 garlic clove, chopped
400 g (14 oz) tinned crushed tomatoes
1 tablespoon tomato paste (concentrated purée)
2 teaspoons chopped dill
extra virgin olive oil, for serving

Filo risotto pie

»PREPARATION 45 MINUTES »COOKING TIME 1 HOUR 45 MINUTES »SERVES 8

2 large red capsicums (peppers)

Risotto

250 ml (9 fl oz/1 cup) white wine
1 litre (35 fl oz/4 cups) vegetable stock
2 tablespoons oil
1 garlic clove, crushed
1 leek, white part only, sliced
1 fennel bulb, thinly sliced
440 g (15½ oz/2 cups) arborio rice
60 g (2¼ oz) freshly grated parmesan cheese
10 sheets filo pastry
60 ml (2 fl oz/¼ cup) olive oil
500 g (1 lb 2 oz) English spinach, blanched
250 g (9 oz) feta cheese, sliced
1 tablespoon sesame seeds

1 Cut the capsicums in half and remove the seeds and membrane. Cut into large, flattish pieces. Grill (broil) until the skin blackens and blisters. Place on a cutting board, cover with a tea towel (dish towel) and allow to cool. Peel the capsicum and chop the flesh.

2 To make the risotto, put the wine and stock in a large saucepan. Bring to the boil and reduce the heat. Heat the oil and garlic in a large heavy-based saucepan. Add the leek and fennel, cook over medium heat for 5 minutes, or until lightly browned. Add the rice and stir for 3 minutes, or until the rice is translucent.

3 Add 250 ml (9 fl oz/1 cup) of the hot stock mixture to the rice and stir until the liquid is absorbed. Add the liquid, 125 ml (4 fl oz/½ cup) at a time, stirring constantly until all the stock has been used and the rice is tender. (This will take about 40 minutes.) Make sure the liquid stays hot as the risotto will become gluggy if it isn't. Remove from the heat, stir in the grated parmesan and season to taste. Set aside until cooled slightly.

4 Preheat the oven to 180°C (350°F/Gas 4). Brush each sheet of filo with the olive oil and fold in half lengthways. Arrange like overlapping spokes on a wheel, in a 23 cm (9 inch) spring-form pan, with one side of pastry hanging over the side of tin.

5 Spoon half the risotto mixture over the pastry and top with half the red capsicum, half the spinach and half the feta. Repeat with the remaining risotto, capsicum, spinach and feta.

6 Fold the pastry over the filling, brush lightly with oil and sprinkle with the sesame seeds. Bake the pie for 50 minutes, or until the pastry is crisp and golden and the filling is heated through.

vegetarian sauces

Creamy chilli dipping sauce

160 g (5¾ oz/⅔ cup) sour cream
3 tablespoons sweet chilli sauce
2 spring onions (scallions), finely chopped
2 tablespoons coriander (cilantro), chopped
1 tablespoon lime juice

1 Put the sour cream in a bowl, add the sweet chilli sauce and stir to combine. Stir in finely chopped spring onions (scallions), chopped coriander (cilantro) and lime juice. Mix well.

2 Chill before serving.

Herb, garlic & yoghurt dipping sauce

200 g (6½ oz) low-fat natural yoghurt
4 tablespoons skim milk
1 teaspoon Dijon mustard
1 tablespoon chives, finely chopped
2 teaspoons fresh parsley, finely chopped
2 teaspoons fresh oregano, chopped
1 clove garlic, crushed

1 Place all the ingredients in a bowl and whisk together. Season with salt and freshly ground black pepper, to taste, then transfer to a serving dish.

2 Chill before serving.

Hummus dipping sauce

425 g (14 oz) can chickpeas
185 ml (6 fl oz/¾ cup) vegetable stock
1 tablespoon tahini paste
2 cloves garlic, chopped
1 teaspoon ground coriander
1 teaspoon ground cumin
2 tablespoons lemon juice

1 Drain the can of chickpeas and put in a food processor with the vegetable stock, tahini paste and chopped garlic.

2 Stir the ground coriander and cumin in a dry frying pan over medium heat for 3 minutes, or until aromatic. Cool slightly, add to the processor and mix until nearly smooth. Mix in the lemon juice.

3 Season with freshly ground black pepper and salt, to taste. If too thick, add a little water.

4 Serve at room temperature.

Peanut sauce

400 ml (14 fl oz) tin coconut milk
2½ tablespoons red curry paste
1 tablespoon tomato paste (purée)
2 tablespoons peanut butter
70 g (2½ oz/½ cup) ground peanuts

1 Take an unshaken 400 ml (14 fl oz) tin of coconut milk and scoop off the thick part that forms at the top (if there is none, just use 3 tablespoons of coconut milk). Put it in a frying pan over medium heat.

2 Add the red curry paste and tomato paste (purée) and stir-fry for 2 minutes, or until aromatic. Add the remaining coconut milk, 2 tablespoons of peanut butter and 70 g (2½ oz/½ cup) of ground peanuts. Simmer gently over low heat, stirring, for 3 minutes.

3 Leave to cool before serving as a dipping sauce or use as a marinade on barbecued vegetable skewers.

Sweet cucumber dipping sauce

3 tablespoons rice vinegar
2 tablespoons sugar
pinch of salt
5 cm (2 inch) piece of cucumber, diced
5 cm (2 inch) piece of carrot, diced
1 tablespoon coriander (cilantro) leaves, finely chopped

1 Put rice vinegar in a small saucepan with sugar and a pinch of salt. Bring slowly to the boil to dissolve the sugar.

2 Leave to cool, then stir in a diced cucumber, diced carrot and finely chopped coriander (cilantro) leaves. Transfer to a serving dish.

Roasted capsicum dipping sauce

2 red capsicums (peppers)
1 teaspoon oil, for frying
2 spring onions, finely chopped
1 tablespoon water
3 tablespoons vegetable stock
2 tablespoons white wine
2 tablespoons tomato paste
¼ teaspoon sugar
1 tablesppon chives, chopped

1 Quarter the capsicums, remove the seeds and membrane and grill (broil) until the skins blister and blacken. Cool under a damp tea towel (dish towel) before peeling. Cut one quarter into thin strips then set aside.

2 Heat the oil in a small pan, add the finely chopped spring onions and water, then stir over heat until the spring onion is soft. Add the remaining capsicum, stock, white wine, tomato paste and sugar. Simmer for 2 minutes, then blend until smooth.

3 Season with freshly ground black pepper and salt, to taste, stir in the chives and garnish with red capsicum strips.

Index

in 2011 by Murdoch Books Pty Limited.

ch Books Australia
/9, 23 Hickson Road, Millers Point NSW 2000
ne: +61 (0)2 8220 2000 Fax: +61 (0)2 8220 2558
w.murdochbooks.com.au

Murdoch Books UK Limited
Erico House, 6th Floor North, 93–99 Upper Richmond Road
Putney, London SW15 2TG
Phone: + 44 (0) 20 8785 5995 Fax: + 44 (0) 20 8785 5985
www.murdochbooks.co.uk

Publisher Lynn Lewis
Design Concept Adam Walker
Designer Katy Wall
Editor Justine Harding
Project Manager Liz Malcolm
Production Joan Beal

National Library of Australia Cataloguing-in-Publication Data:
Title: Vegetarian.
ISBN: 978-1-74266-418-7 (pbk.)
Series: Test kitchen favourites.
Notes: Includes index.
Subjects: Vegetarian cooking.
Dewey Number: 641.5636

Printed by 1010 Printing International Limited, China.